FREUD FOR ARCHITECTS

Freud for Architects explains what Freud offers to the understanding of architectural creativity and architectural experience, with case examples from early modern architecture to the present.

Freud's observations on the human psyche and its influence on culture and social behavior have generated a great deal of discussion since the 19th century. Yet, what Freud's key ideas offer to the understanding of architectural creativity and experience has received little direct attention. That is partly because Freud opened the door to a place where conventional research in architecture has little traction, the unconscious. Adding to the difficulties, Freud's collection of work is vast and daunting. *Freud for Architects* navigates Freud's key ideas and bridges a chasm between architecture and psychoanalytic theory.

The book highlights Freud's ideas on the foundational developments of childhood, developments on which the adult psyche is based. It explains why and how the developmental stages could influence adult architectural preferences and preoccupations, spatial intuition, and beliefs about what is proper and right for architectural design. As such, *Freud for Architects* will be of great interest to students, practitioners, and scholars in a range of disciplines including architecture, psychoanalysis, and philosophy.

John Abell, PhD, specializes in modern architectural design and critical theory, particularly as these intersect with aesthetic experience, material craft, and design technologies.

Thinkers for Architects

Series Editor: Adam Sharr, Newcastle University, UK

Editorial Board

Jonathan A. Hale, University of Nottingham, UK
Hilde Heynen, KU Leuven, Netherlands
David Leatherbarrow, University of Pennsylvania, USA

Architects have often looked to philosophers and theorists from beyond the discipline for design inspiration or in search of a critical framework for practice. This original series offers quick, clear introductions to key thinkers who have written about architecture and whose work can yield insights for designers.

"Each unintimidatingly slim book makes sense of the subjects' complex theories."
Building Design

"… a valuable addition to any studio space or computer lab."
Architectural Record

"… a creditable attempt to present their subjects in a useful way."
Architectural Review

Virilio for Architects
John Armitage

Peirce for Architects
Richard Coyne

Merleau-Ponty for Architects
Jonathan Hale

Baudrillard for Architects
Francesco Proto

Kant for Architects
Diane Morgan

Freud for Architects
John Abell

For more information about this series, please visit: https://www.routledge.com/thinkers-for-architects/book-series/thinkarch

THINKERS FOR ARCHITECTS

Freud for Architects

John Abell

LONDON AND NEW YORK

First published 2021
by Routledge
2 Park Square, Milton Park, Abingdon, Oxon OX14 4RN

and by Routledge
52 Vanderbilt Avenue, New York, NY 10017

Routledge is an imprint of the Taylor & Francis Group, an informa business

© 2021 John Abell

The right of John Abell to be identified as author of this work has been asserted by him in accordance with sections 77 and 78 of the Copyright, Designs and Patents Act 1988.

All rights reserved. No part of this book may be reprinted or reproduced or utilized in any form or by any electronic, mechanical, or other means, now known or hereafter invented, including photocopying and recording, or in any information storage or retrieval system, without permission in writing from the publishers.

Trademark notice: Product or corporate names may be trademarks or registered trademarks and are used only for identification and explanation without intent to infringe.

British Library Cataloguing-in-Publication Data
A catalogue record for this book is available from the British Library

Library of Congress Cataloging-in-Publication Data

Names: Abell, John (John H.), author.
Title: Freud for architects/John Abell.
Description: New York : Routledge, 2020. | Series: Thinkers for architects |
Includes bibliographical references and index.
Identifiers: LCCN 2020025080 (print) | LCCN 2020025081 (ebook) |
ISBN 9781138390676 (hardback) | ISBN 9781138390683 (paperback) |
ISBN 9780429423253 (ebook)
Subjects: LCSH: Freud, Sigmund, 1856-1939. | Architecture—Philosophy.
Classification: LCC BF109.F74 A64 2021 (print) | LCC BF109.F74 (ebook) |
DDC 150.19/5402472—dc23
LC record available at https://lccn.loc.gov/2020025080
LC ebook record available at https://lccn.loc.gov/2020025081

ISBN: 978-1-138-39067-6 (hbk)
ISBN: 978-1-138-39068-3 (pbk)
ISBN: 978-0-429-42325-3 (ebk)

Typeset in Frutiger
by KnowledgeWorks Global Ltd.

Contents

Series editor's preface	viii
List of illustrations	x
Acknowledgments	xi

1. Introduction   1

> The psyche, aesthetic experience, and architecture 2
> Reading Freud, psychoanalytic theory, and clinical practice 6
> Social influence, psychotherapeutic design, wild analysis,
> and architectural "aeffects" 9
> Outline of the book 13

2. Freud and modernity: selfhood and emancipatory self-determination   17

> Freud and Vienna: modernity and culture 18
> Contrasting architectural preferences in *fin-de-siècle* Vienna 19
> *The Interpretation of Dreams*, 1900 20
> Psychical selfhood and self-determination 22
> Trauma, repression, architecture of screen memories, remembering,
> repeating, and working through 24
> Cultural screens, disconnection, negation, and affirmation 32
> Conclusion 35

3. Aesthetic experience: the object, empathy, the unconscious,
   and architectural design   37

> Unconsciously projecting oneself and intuiting the shape
> or form of an art object: Semper, Vischer, Schmarsow,
> Wölfflin, Giedion, and Moholy-Nagy 38

Stone and phantasy, smooth and rough 44
Inside-outside corners, birth trauma, and character armor 48
The turbulent section and the paranoid critical method 50
Asymmetric blur zones and the uncanny 51
Conclusion 53

4. Open form, the formless, and "that oceanic feeling" 54

Architectural formlessness, not literal formlessness 54
Freud and the spatialities of the psychical apparatus 57
Phases of psychical development in childhood 58
The oral phase 60
Repression 61
Blurred zones and architectural empathy for formlessness 62
Conclusion 67

5. Closed-form, rule-based composition and control of the architectural gift 68

The second phase of development, the anal phase, and struggles
over control of a gift 68
Threshold practices: isolation, repetition, procedures for handling
objects, and diverting impulses 71
A brief history of closed-form, rule-based composition and control
of the architectural gift 72
House II 75
Conclusion 78

6. Architectural simulation: wishful phantasy and the real 79

The third phase of development, the phallic phase, a wish and
overcoming prohibitions against the wish 82
Simulation, wishes, and world views 84
"Vertical horizon" and the plot of phallic phantasy 87
Conclusion 90

7. Spaces of social encounter: freedoms and constraints — 92

The last phase of development in childhood, the genital phase, and the search for obtainable objects 95
Open slab versus regime room: empathy for freedom versus constraint in spaces of social encounter 100
Conclusion 103

Conclusion — 105

Further reading — 108
References — 110
Index — 117

Series editor's preface

Adam Sharr

Architects have often looked to thinkers in philosophy and theory for design ideas or in search of a critical framework for practice. Yet architects and students of architecture can struggle to navigate thinkers' writings. It can be daunting to approach original texts with little appreciation of their contexts. And existing introductions seldom explore a thinker's architectural material in any detail. This original series offers clear, quick, and accurate introductions to key thinkers who have written about architecture. Each book summarizes what a thinker has to offer for architects. It locates their architectural thinking in the body of their work, introduces significant books and essays, helps decode terms, and provides quick reference for further reading. If you find philosophical and theoretical writing about architecture difficult, or just don't know where to begin, this series will be indispensable.

Books in the *Thinkers for Architects* series come out of architecture. They pursue architectural modes of understanding, aiming to introduce a thinker to an architectural audience. Each thinker has a unique and distinctive ethos, and the structure of each book derives from the character at its focus. The thinkers explored are prodigious writers, and any short introduction can only address a fraction of their work. Each author – an architect or an architectural critic – has focused on a selection of a thinker's writings that they judge most relevant to designers and interpreters of architecture. Inevitably, much will be left out.

These books will be the first point of reference, rather than the last word, about a particular thinker for architects. It is hoped that these books will encourage you to read further, offering an incentive to delve deeper into the original writings of the thinker being introduced.

The *Thinkers for Architects* series has proved highly successful over more than a decade, expanding now to 17 volumes dealing with familiar cultural figures whose writings have influenced architectural designers, critics, and commentators in distinctive and important ways. Books explore the work of Gilles Deleuze and Felix Guattari; Martin Heidegger; Luce Irigaray; Homi Bhabha; Pierre Bourdieu; Walter Benjamin; Jacques Derrida; Hans-Georg Gadamer, Michael Foucault, Nelson Goodman, Henri Lefebvre, Paul Virilio, Maurice Merleau-Ponty, Immanuel Kant, Charles Sanders Peirce, Jean Baudrillard, and now Sigmund Freud. The series continues to expand, addressing an increasingly rich diversity of thinkers who have something to say to architects.

Adam Sharr is Head of the School of Architecture, Planning and Landscape at Newcastle University; Editor-in-Chief of *arq: Architectural Research Quarterly*, a Cambridge University Press international architecture journal; and Principal of Adam Sharr Architects. His books published by Routledge include *Heidegger for Architects* and *Reading Architecture and Culture*.

Illustrations

2. Freud and modernity: selfhood and emancipatory self-determination
   1. "The Architecture of Hysteria," Sigmund Freud, 1897, redrawn: memory-scenes and depth of repression. Triangles represent "Symptoms" e.g., memory scenes, phantasies. Dashed lines, arrows, and numbers represent the paths of psychoanalytic "Work" uncovering the connections (solid lines) between symptoms and depths of repression I, II, III, IV. 28
4. Open form, the formless, and "that oceanic feeling"
   2. Closed form versus "space relationships," László Moholy-Nagy, 1928, redrawn: intuition of open form and formlessness. 55
   3. Blurred zone buildings, Rebstockpark masterplan, Peter Eisenman, 2003, redrawn: architectural empathy for formlessness, not literal formlessness. 63
   4. Plan, blurred zone matrix, Rebstockpark, Peter Eisenman, 2003, redrawn: a "realm of the unconscious where desire operates." 65
5. Closed-form, rule-based composition and control of the architectural gift
   5. House II diagrams, Peter Eisenman, 1969–1970, redrawn: rule-based composition. 69
6. Architectural simulation: wishful phantasy and the real
   6. "Vertical Horizon," Daniel Libeskind, 1979, detail, area of detail indicated by square immediately above with dashed line around lower left corner, redrawn: wishful architectural simulation. 80
7. Spaces of social encounter: freedoms and constraints
   7. Educatorium, plan of first floor showing ground floor areas beyond, Rem Koolhaas/OMA, 1997, redrawn: open areas (A) versus regime rooms (B) 94

Acknowledgments

My research on *Freud for Architects* began at the Architectural Association in London while working on what would eventually become my PhD dissertation. Returning to the topic for papers, conference presentations, and this book provided opportunities to develop and present new material here. For that, most recently, I am grateful to Adam Sharr and Fran Ford at Routledge. I would like to express my deep gratitude to Mark Cousins at the Architectural Association, who patiently helped me see how to take a psychoanalytic idea and do some work with it. Andrew Benjamin, Paul Hirst, Gordana Korolija, Lawrence Barth, and Simos Yannas also helped me think more clearly about important aspects of the topic along the way. I have also benefited from conversations with Lorens Holm and from his published work on Jacques Lacan and architecture. I would also like to thank Alexus Castaneda for the drawings in this book.

CHAPTER 1

Introduction

Freud for Architects is intended as an introductory guide for architecture students, architects, and readers who are generally interested in the psychology of design. The aim is to outline how Freud's thought helps explain aesthetic experience in architecture and design preferences, particularly preferences associated with unconventional and experimental architecture, which is often simply called "avant-garde" architecture.

Freud is so much a part of modern popular culture that some of his ideas are taken for granted in everyday life. Dreams, slips of the tongue, and jokes are commonly taken to have psychological double meanings, potentially embarrassing meanings that somehow, tantalizingly, also pique interest in them. Marketing campaigns and social media, consistently and knowingly, appeal to the self-centered tendencies of the human psyche that are otherwise often called narcissistic tendencies. Film and television routinely incorporate sexuality, celebrating the human capacity for sexual feelings and desires while fostering audience identification with characters. Social groups, professional disciplines, and workplace teams routinely reflect the influence of group psychology, typically involving a leader and inclusion-exclusion behaviors that reinforce the leader and group behavior. A head of state unwittingly and unconsciously follows the oedipal playbook when he says to his illicit lover, "you remind me of my daughter (Cooper, 2018; Lee, 2019)." Increasingly, personal pronouns, e.g., he, him, his, she, her, hers, are acknowledged to be matters of personal sexual preference and identity choice rather than genital inheritance.

With *The Interpretation of Dreams*, 1900, Freud's thought has greatly influenced the popular understanding of the personal and subjective aspects of self. During his lifetime, 1856–1939, Freud established a highly influential and emancipatory modern theory of selfhood, while generating a great deal of debate (Zaretsky, 2015: 36). Indeed, Freud remains a major influence on a system of thought that links different kinds of human experience to different ways of being human, that is, a system of thought on selfhood and self-determination, which, in all of its variety, has been credited with supporting the modern liberal democratic state, and yet has also been leveraged to support oppressive ideologies (Marks, 2017: 8).

Despite the prominence of Freud's thought, what his key ideas offer to the understanding of architectural experience and creativity has received little direct attention. That is partly because Freud opened the door to a place where conventional research in architecture has little traction, the unconscious. Adding to the difficulties, Freud's collection of work is vast and daunting. *Freud for Architects* introduces Freud's key ideas, navigating the terrain between architecture and Freud's thought, and focuses on ideas that are particularly relevant to architecture and aesthetic experience.

The psyche, aesthetic experience, and architecture

Though well established in the arts and humanities as one of the pillars of thought on subjective aspects of selfhood, Freud's thought has a rather obscure connection to architecture and what architecture generically refers to as the "designer" and the "user." When considering the human experience of architecture, architects and architecture students are far more familiar with ways of thinking about the human experience that stem from the experience of one's own body in architectural settings, an awareness that phenomenology and phenomenologists have focused on. For example, phenomenologists such as Immanuel Kant (1724–1804), Martin Heidegger (1889–1976), or Jacques Merleau-Ponty (1908–1961), who focused on the conscious experience of the physical body and the senses, help architecture deepen its understanding of human experience. That is partly because body experience offers a straightforward way to describe and interpret the physical experience of a building and its parts (see, for example, *The Eyes of the Skin*, Juhani Pallasmaa, 2012). Phenomenologists have also suggested that daydreams and childhood memories influence adult physical experience (Gaston Bachelard, *The Poetics of Space*, 1969) and, further, that relations with objects in childhood influence the creation and experience of geometry in adulthood (Edmund Husserl, *The Origin of Geometry*, 1970). Yet the core psychical memories, body experiences, and objects in childhood upon which adult experience is based have remained elusive to phenomenologists. Thus, phenomenology aims to describe the direct experience of objects but lacks a psychical basis for understanding body experience, particularly when viewed from a psychoanalytic perspective (Cousins, 1996). Similarly, among the many important insights inspired by Freud's thought is the insight that human experience and human selfhood are more multidimensional than a correlation of physical body experience to architecture can account for. The same holds for the influence of Gestalt psychology on architecture and its influence on the understanding of the visual experience of the building facade. Some building facades, or a large part of a façade, are mainly transparent glass such that one sees through a glass façade into the building. In contrast, some façades imply outer surface to inner depth relationships rather than literally reveal those relationships. Based on the influence of Gestalt psychology, those relationships have long been known in architecture as the difference between "literal transparency" and on the other hand "phenomenal transparency."

Drawing on Gestalt psychology, Colin Rowe (1920–1999), an architecture historian and theorist, and Robert Slutzky (1929–2005), a painter and architecture theorist, called attention to the innate human capacity to grasp and appreciate building façade designs that imply rather than literally reveal outer surface to inner depth relationships. They defined that aspect of façade design as "phenomenal transparency" in contrast to literal transparency. The garden façade of Villa Stein-de-Monzie, Garches, by Le Corbusier, 1926, is a case in point. There, Rowe and Slutsky note, a relatively shallow layer of volumetric depth and structure behind the façade are implied by a visual pattern of façade elements: there is a flat area of the façade with horizontal "ribbon windows" above the ground floor; there is the recessed area of the façade below on the ground floor; walls that define the left and right sides of the building when viewed from the garden also provide visual cues; and a deep void on the left side of the façade suggests the actual depth of the building. The relationships imply a shallow band of space behind the ribbon windows, yet the deep void suggests actual depth. The relationships establish a phenomenal transparency, rather than literal transparency. The façade of the workshop wing of the Bauhaus building by Gropius, 1925–1926, is an example of a literally transparent façade. There, one literally sees through transparent glass into the physical depth behind the façade. The visual relationships are literally revealed by the façade (Rowe and Slutzky, 1963). Yet, Rowe and Slutzky do not take up questions concerning why 2 people looking at the same façade, either a literally transparent façade or a phenomenally transparent façade, might have contrasting reactions, one finding it to be a favorable aesthetic experience and other finding it uninteresting if not "annoying" and unpleasurable. Freud hinted at this kind of issue in, "Findings, Ideas, Problems," written in 1941 near the end of his life, he wrote,

> **Space may be the projection of the extension of the psychical apparatus. No other derivation is probable. Instead of Kant's a priori determinants of our psychical apparatus. Psyche is extended....**

> (Freud, 1941: 300)

That is to say, human experience is always influenced by the projection of the internal psyche outward onto relations with objects in the external world. Building on that idea, *Freud for Architects* explains what Freud offers to the understanding of architecture by explaining how the psyche is extended, helping to explain architectural design preferences, creativity, and architectural experience, with examples from early modern architecture to the present. The examples also highlight how Freud's ideas can be applied to analyze and interpret design and to interpret design criticism, with emphasis on the formal qualities of design. Examples are representative of particular kinds of formal expression in architecture, mainly "open form" and "closed form." Each has a unique spatiality. For example, closed form is closed to the outside and what is beyond an enclosing wall. In contrast, the spatiality of an open form is physically open to what is outside, and the emphasis in relationships between a building's interior and site and site context is on continuity rather than discontinuity.

Insofar as each architectural example presented in *Freud for Architects* represents a type of expression, e.g., closed form or open form, the analysis and insights in each case are in principle transferable to other similar cases.

...human experience is always influenced by the projection of the internal psyche outward onto relations with objects in the external world.

Freud's observations on the human psyche help explain the aesthetic preferences of the architect, client, and group audiences for architecture. The special focus in *Freud for Architects* is on designs that raise our awareness of conventions by challenging conventions, often simply called avant-garde designs. The examples help explain why, psychologically, any architect's formal preferences might align – or not – with consumer preferences, e.g., clients, users, critical flock of followers, or detractors. Likewise, the examples offer insights into unconscious motivations that lay behind attraction to, and avoidance of, formal characteristics of designs, e.g., open form and closed form. The examples also offer insights into discussions that fuel architecture debates, including concerns for conventional design versus "the new" or avant-garde design; debates on what defines architecture and what is "proper" for architecture versus what is "outside" of architecture or beyond the boundaries of architecture; and debates on whether building designs that emphasize the expression of constructed elements and how they join are more praiseworthy than building designs that emphasize ornamentation or surface-effects such as phenomenal transparency.

Another reason why Freud's thought has a rather obscure connection to architecture and what architecture generically refers to as the "designer" and the "user" is that introductory history courses in architecture school often describe building design in terms of style changes driven by social and technological changes. Similarly, historical time periods are defined by social conditions and technological conditions of a time period: different social concerns and different technologies. Thus, the social and technological influences on the designer and the user of one time period are, logically, different than another time period, and so too architecture style and architectural experience, it is supposed, are different.

A concern drawn from psychoanalytic theory is that when architecture histories and theories focus narrowly on social and technological conditions, they overlook the human psyche and indeed are not sufficiently mindful of human experience and selfhood. Nonetheless, social and technological conditions do act on something and leave their stamp on something: a person. Ignoring that does not make the problem go away (Cousins and Hussain, 1984: 254–256). Others have described that shortcoming as the difference between a "thick" (psychoanalytic) view of selfhood versus a "thin" view (Gay, 2000: 2–4). In raising these issues here, the aim is not to dismiss the histories and theories of architecture taught in architecture schools. Rather, the aim is to suggest what Freud offers to the understanding of style, aesthetic expression, aesthetic experience, designer, and user, beyond what architecture history and theory courses typically offer.

Reading Freud, psychoanalytic theory, and clinical practice

There are a number of general introductory reference books on Freud's work. Freud himself gave "Introductory Lectures on Psychoanalysis" between 1915 and 1917 and supplemented them in 1933 with "New Introductory Lectures." Freud's introductory lectures are compiled along with his entire body of work, and many letters to colleagues, in 23 hardcover volumes titled *The Standard Edition of the Complete Psychological Works of Sigmund Freud*, translated from German and edited by James Strachey and Freud's daughter, Anna Freud, who was also a psychoanalyst. The last volume of the *Standard Edition*, *SE XXIV*, contains useful indexes and bibliographies for the entire collection. The *Standard Edition* is widely regarded as the primary and authoritative source on Freud's thought and as the proper source for scholarly citation. However,

Penguin Books offers a Freud Library series of 15 paperback books that is widely available, conveniently sized, and contains what are generally regarded as Freud's key works reprinted from the *Standard Edition*. Further, *The Freud Reader*, by Gay, 1989, W.W. Norton & Company Ltd., New York, is perhaps most useful as a general reference for the newcomer because it presents a chronological selection of Freud's works, drawn from the *Standard Edition*, under helpful section titles such as "Classic Theory," "Therapy and Technique," and "Psychoanalysis in Culture," highlighting content areas that are not obvious in the *Standard Edition*. The compilations mentioned here are for a general readership, and Freud's thought is not condensed or described in a way that makes his thought more readily accessible to the architect and specifically relevant to architectural issues. However, perusing Freud's writings repays the effort because it reveals that Freud was an eloquent writer and compelling thinker who was mindful of the reader, sometimes by necessity communicating ideas to a psychoanalytic audience, at other times addressing a wider readership. Nonetheless, because Freud's thought developed incrementally over time, he often refers to his previous publications, such that one of his papers inevitably leads the reader to his other papers, which altogether requires a committed and persistent reader. *Freud for Architects* highlights key ideas with the goal of rendering Freud accessible to the architect who has little or no prior experience with Freud other than perhaps terms or phrases that routinely find expression in popular culture.

...perusing Freud's writings repays the effort because it reveals Freud was an eloquent writer and compelling thinker who was mindful of the reader...

In the main, Freud's thought concerns the universal core developments of childhood upon which the adult psyche is based. He came to believe developmental phases influence debilitating psychological disorders in adulthood, as well as a "normal" range of behaviors, expressed by preferences and preoccupations, spatial intuitions, dreams, anxieties, avoidances, obsessions, repressions of childhood thoughts and experiences, and symbolic condensations and displacements of memory images. Two of Freud's key works on the developments of childhood and related ideas are: *Three Essays on Sexuality*, 1905 (1920), which Freud continually revised, and *The Ego and The Id*, 1923. Freud also made compelling observations on art, literature, and culture. The *Psychopathology of Everyday Life*, 1901, *Creative Writers and Daydreaming*, 1908, and *Civilization and its Discontents*, 1930, are among the most widely read and accessible of Freud's works.

Freud's thought concerns the universal core developments of childhood upon which the adult psyche is based. He came to believe developmental phases influence debilitating psychological disorders in adulthood, as well as a "normal" range of behaviors…

Understanding Freud's relevance to architecture also involves making a distinction between Freud's contributions to psychoanalytic theory today as a body of knowledge versus psychoanalysis as a clinical practice. Freud's works provide the theoretical foundation for the psychoanalyst today, works the psychoanalyst must read (ed. Phillips, 2006: 1). One of the subtle and overlooked aspects of Freud's continuing importance is that psychoanalytic theory stands on firmer ground scientifically than the clinical practice of psychoanalysis. Clinical practices vary widely, influenced by combining different approaches with different emphasis, resulting in psychotherapeutic hybrids without a common guiding rubric for therapeutic technique (Marks, 2017: 5). Thus, clinical practices struggle with science-based expectations for mapping clinical results with evidence-based research strategies. Nonetheless, neuroscience researchers acknowledge that the unconscious influences emotions and thought processes and suggest that there is a neurological basis for at least some aspects of Freud's theory on the unconscious (Weston, 2002. Kandel, 2012). Certainly, neuroscience is gaining traction as a model for design thinking, particularly with regard to the brain's neurological embodiment of the body. For example, Harry Mallgrave, the noted architecture historian, in *The Architect's Brain* writes, "the neurons in the big toe are as much a part of our brain as the frontal lobe that allows us to think about our big toe. The brain is the body in all of its workings and vice versa" (Mallgrave, 2011, 135). Remarkably for the understanding of the architect's psyche, or anyone else's psyche, Freud long ago reasoned that emotional contents and processes of the adult unconscious are linked to the primary sensory organs of childhood. However, efforts to apply Freud's ideas should mind the cautionary as well as promising distinctions outlined above. On one side is the caution stemming from the natural sciences and cognitive science that psychoanalysis as a field of knowledge is soft scientifically. On the other side is the promising distinction that Freud and psychoanalytic theory offer insightful and nuanced descriptions of the human psyche and human behavior.

Social influence, psychotherapeutic design, wild analysis, and architectural "aeffects"

In the first half of the 20th century, Freud's thought and clinical practice gained support from individual affluent clients, initially mostly women, but increasingly his thought defined psychoanalysis as a discipline of knowledge and influenced the general understanding of the human psyche well beyond his native Vienna. His thought was developed, transmitted, and transformed through association with an inner circle of colleagues, clients, publication and translation of his papers, professional associations and visitations, extending internationally and most visibly in major cities of Europe, Argentina, and the United States, and by authoritarian as well as neoliberal governments in support of ideological and social aims (Gay, 1988. Grosskurth, 1991. Zaretsky, 2004. Damousi & Plotkin,

2009. Marks, 2017. Marks 2018). Socially minded "free clinics" arose to offer psychoanalytic counseling to the public in Vienna and Berlin in the 1920s, and in the Harlem neighborhood of New York City in 1945 (Danto 2009: 30–38. Danto 2005. Zaretsky 2015: 128). Freud's son, Ernst Freud, in Berlin early in the 1920s, was perhaps the first architect to design a public psychotherapy clinic characterized by simple, clear, open-plan arrangements (Danto 2009: 36. Volker, 2011). Ernst had studied with Richard Neutra in Vienna under the well-known modernist architect Adolf Loos. Much later, after having immigrated to the United States and settling in southern California, Neutra applied the ideas of the socially revolutionary psychoanalyst Wilhelm Reich to design residences. Reich, as a young psychoanalyst, had gained professional experience in Freud's free clinic in Vienna. In 1939, Reich emigrated from Austria to the United States, fleeing Nazi aggression. Neutra designed Reich-inspired residences with open-plan areas including open and transparent corners intended to blur distinctions between inside and outside and to relieve emotional and sexual tension (Lavin, 2007). Essentially, Neutra applied Reich's ideas to design residences to affect his clients in a way that would reduce internal stress before reaching harmful levels.

Neutra's open-corner designs are generally regarded as praiseworthy historic examples of modern architecture, aside from mental health benefits Neutra or his clients might have supposed the designs provided. As architectural interpretations of Reich's ideas, Neutra's designs raise interesting questions about the ways Freud's system of thought can be reliably applied to architecture and indeed has been applied. Reich is interesting, too, partly because he came to believe in radical measures for preventing mental disorders as opposed to their treatment after they arise. Neutra believed he could draw on Reich's ideas to increase architecture's agency, to increase the performance of a residence by designing it to promote the mental health of its occupants. Yet Reich's psychoanalytic eccentricities put him at odds with Freud and psychoanalysis as a body of knowledge. Those issues will be taken up in Chapter 3; the aim here is simply to foreground an example of the architectural interpretation of psychoanalytic ideas and the issue of reliability in the application of Freud's thought to architecture.

Freud's use of psychoanalytic concepts to interpret culture, literature, and works of art certainly warrants further application to interpret architecture and aesthetic experience. However, Freud would perhaps call some efforts "wild analysis," as when he cautioned against psychoanalytic diagnosis of a patient's symptoms by anyone who is not actually a psychoanalyst (Freud, 1910: 226). Nevertheless, clinical diagnosis aside, Freud's ideas have been reliably and fruitfully applied by many who are not psychoanalysts to interpret creative work in the arts and humanities, in some cases in support of emancipatory aims. For example, some in architecture have applied Freudian concepts to break free of art-historical conventions that they viewed as too restrictive, particularly the longstanding Vitruvian convention that architecture should mirror an idealized physical body of the adult male. Important examples of applying Freudian concepts to break free of such constraints are *Blurred Zones*, 2003, by Peter Eisenman and *Delirious New York*, by Rem Koolhaas, 1997, examples that will be developed further in Chapters 3 and 4.

Problematically, Freud and psychoanalysis have been leveraged in the 20th century by fascist regimes in support of nationalistic, authoritarian, and racist agendas (Damousi and Plotkin, 2012: xvii. Pasqualini, 2012: 21). Also problematically, some in the arts and humanities have drawn from Freud and psychoanalysis to interpret artistic production that conflicts with established norms and ideals and to judge nonconforming designs or styles as deviant, if not perverse, e.g., *The End of Art*, 2004, and "The Spirit of Business, the Business of Spirit: The Postmodern Quandary of the Museum," 1993, both by Donald Kuspit. Yet, as the fine arts lecturer and psychoanalyst Lucille Holmes cautions, Kuspit's judgments and generalizations contradict what Freud actually said about what is normal psychologically (Holmes, 2012: 1). Indeed, Freud maintained that "an unbroken chain bridges the gap between the neuroses in all their manifestations and normality." And what some might view as perversion "is itself of no rarity but must form a part of what passes as the normal constitution" (Freud, 1905 (1920): 171). With those caveats in mind, Freud offers viable psychoanalytic insights on how the unconscious might influence architectural experience and design. Certainly, Freud is the common thread running through architecture literature that draws from psychoanalytic theory to explain the aesthetic experience, including work drawing from Freud's contemporaries and successors.

...architectural design can be experienced as a vaguely familiar affirmation of unconscious wishes, and on the other hand experienced as an unwelcome and, thus, ugly reminder of unconscious wishes...

Mark Cousins, a cultural critic and architecture theorist, writes that Freud and psychoanalytic theory help explain how architectural design can be experienced as a vaguely familiar affirmation of unconscious wishes, and on the other hand experienced as an unwelcome and, thus, ugly reminder of unconscious wishes. In the latter case, the architectural affect is such that one feels something about the design "is there and should not be," and where architecture becomes a scene and dramatic "zone of representation" of unconscious experiences (Cousins, 1994: 63). For Freud, that zone of representation would arise as a "projection of...the psychical apparatus" (Freud, 1941: 300), a projection involving architecture. Viewing the challenging designs of well-known architects through the lens of Freud's thought helps explain human empathy for architecture and helps explain converging and diverging preferences for architectural design. In such cases, Cousins, (2005) would perhaps agree, it can be difficult to distinguish between an architect expressing unconscious wishes through design (architectural effect, the idea that designs are the result of unconscious wishes); or what one might suppose another's experience of the design would be (supposed-affect, for example, what the architect imagines a person's experience of the design would be); or someone's actual experience influenced by their projection of unconscious ideas onto a design (affect, or experience influenced by the projection of unconscious ideas onto a design). Similarly, the psychical relationship between the architect and the architect's building design is a relationship of effects and affects, or more precisely, a matter of "aeffects."

Outline of the book

Chapter 1 outlines the general relevance of Freud's thought in popular culture, psychoanalysis, and architecture. Freud advanced the idea that the psyche is a kind of internal structure or "apparatus" that is projected onto the external world. Human relations with objects in the external world, whether the object is another person or a building, can be expected to express the ways the psychical apparatus is projected. Thus, the outward projection of the psyche can be expected to influence architectural creativity and architectural experience. Efforts to design architectural settings, for example, the design of a treatment clinic or a residence, highlight subtle but important differences in architectural aims with regard to Freud's thought. First, there is the idea that architectural design is influenced by the outward projection of an internal psychical apparatus. In this case, architecture, perhaps a building, arises as an effect of the psyche. Second is the idea that architectural experience expresses the outward projection of an internal psychical apparatus. Third is the idea that architecture can be designed to support psychical well-being. In the latter case, the design of the architectural setting is tailored, one supposes, to the needs of the psychical apparatus. In the case of residential designs by the architect Richard Neutra, the design of the architectural setting is tailored to affect the psychical apparatus in a way that would reduce internal stress before reaching harmful levels. The ideas and examples in Chapter 1 highlight Freud's influence on the understanding of a range of issues concerning the psyche and architecture. Chapter 1 concludes with a notion outlined in the introduction above, that relationships between the internal psychical apparatus and the objects of aesthetic experience are relationships defined by effects, affects, and aeffects.

Chapter 2, on Freud and modernity, selfhood, and emancipatory self-determination, begins with Freud's development of his psychoanalytic theory in the historical context of Vienna at the turn of the century. This serves as a basis for introducing and expanding on Freud's key ideas while also staking out his clinical and cultural observations in that historical context. Psychoanalysis itself, as a clinical practice and as a body of knowledge, was a liberating outgrowth of social upheavals in late 19th-century Vienna, not the cause of the upheavals at that time. While Freud viewed his efforts as scientific efforts, by interpreting subjective experiences in everyday life he offered influential perspectives on the emancipatory promises of modernity. The chapter outlines Freud's influential views on sexuality, identity, unconscious, trauma, repression, and therapeutic technique involving remembering, repeating, and working through trauma. Freud's "Architecture of Hysteria" diagram (1897) of memory-scenes and layers of repression sums up how screen memories mask and resist the memory of traumatic experience. Those ideas have long functioned as tools to think psychoanalytically and to analyze social and cultural phenomena. Those tools are applied in Chapter 2 to explore architecture studio culture myths and taboos and types of potentially traumatic studio experience. The chapter also outlines how the African-American writer Richard Wright applied Freud's ideas to explore the behavioral and cultural experiences of racism and the cultural screens of racism.

Chapter 3, on the aesthetic experience of objects, empathy, unconscious, and architectural design, introduces Freud's influence on architecture thinkers, particularly his influence on questions concerning the aesthetic experience. The chapter introduces how architectural designers and theorists have sought to understand aesthetic intuition, how people unconsciously experience and identify with architecture, and what leads to pleasing or displeasing experience. The discussion begins with a key example before Freud, Gottfried Semper's "principle of dressing" (1860), and then introduces "empathy theory" at the turn of the 20th century with Robert Vischer's notion of "empathy," whereby one "unconsciously" wraps oneself in the contours of an object "as in a garment" (1873). A cross-section of key ideas on architectural experience since Vischer highlights contrasting perspectives on the virtues of closed form versus open form, raising questions about how Freud's ideas can be reliably applied to interpret architecture.

Chapter 4, on open form, the formless, and "that oceanic feeling," is the first of 4 chapters exploring Freud's key ideas on how the structure of the psyche develops in each phase of psychical development in childhood. The chapter draws from Freud's thought on the first phase of development in childhood, the oral phase, to explain the architectural empathy for open form, the formless, and "oceanic" feelings of oneness with the world. Freud said, early in the first phase of development, the child does not distinguish between itself and the external world. In that sense, the adult standing by the sea who experiences oceanic feelings of oneness with the world is experiencing a residue of selfhood in the oral phase of childhood or rather self-identity in that phase. Thus, adult oceanic feelings recall a kind of formlessness in the first phase where the infant does not distinguish between the "external world" and "self." That earliest experience of selfhood has fascinating implications for the understanding of architectural preferences for open form and the formless. Chapter 4 examines 2 examples from early 20th-century modern architecture, Sigfried Giedion's fascination with open form in modern architecture (1928 and 1941) and László Moholy-Nagy's exploration of "space relations" (1928). The chapter then examines a much more recent example, a "blurred zone," by Peter Eisenman, 1990–1991.

Chapter 5 explores the architectural empathy for closed form, rule-based composition, and control issues associated with viewing architectural design as a "gift" the architect shares with clients. The chapter draws from Freud's thought on the third phase of development in childhood, the anal phase. Freud notes that the defining experiences of selfhood in that phase are such that the child identifies closely with a special object that the child regards as a "gift" and hoards the gift. Struggles for control of the gift involve conditions or rules for dealing with it and ultimately involve ambivalence toward the special gift object. Logically, closed form in architecture contrasts with open form and formless. Closed form emphasizes limits and a clearly defined framework, as well as thresholds that separate the architectural object from other objects and that internally divide the object. The chapter focuses on one compelling modern example of empathy for closed form and rule-based composition, and the control of the architectural gift: the "House II" project by Peter Eisenman, 1969–1970.

Chapter 6, on architectural simulation and wishful fantasy, draws from what Freud calls "phantasy" as a defining experience of selfhood in the third phase of development in childhood, the phallic phase. "Phantasy" is a psychoanalytic term for a fantasy that involves wish fulfillment, particularly wish fulfillment in relation to obstacles against fulfillment in the external world. In the phallic phantasy, the child casts itself in a phallic role, a role in which prohibitions against impulses toward a special object of affection in the external "real" world can be overcome, whereby the child has the object of affection in the way that the child wants it. Freud's observations help explain fantasy-based architecture and reality-based architecture as contrasting categories of architectural simulation and the empathy for each as contrasting though not mutually exclusive categories of aesthetic experience. Logically, architectural design is wishful if not a propositional act. Design simulation, with traditional media or digital media, has long enabled the architect to transfer wishful ideas in the mind's eye to graphic representations of ideas that can be shared with others in the external world and to challenge architecture convention. In Chapter 6, "Vertical Horizon" by architect Daniel Libeskind, 1979, is the primary architectural example. The drawing indulges fancifully in the freedoms afforded by simulation to overcome architectural conventions, prohibitions, and taboos. In that sense, simulation can position the architect in the phallic role of having an architectural object of affection in the way the architect wants it, in spite of prohibitions in the external world against it.

Chapter 7, on the empathy for spaces of social encounter and their freedoms and constraints, draws from Freud's observations on the last phase of development in childhood, the genital phase. The Educatorium by Koolhaas/ OMA, 1997, Utrecht, The Netherlands, is a key example in the chapter, illustrating how architects employ the elements of architecture to define social freedoms as well as constraints in spaces of social encounter. The Educatorium helps explain how modern institutions and architecture (e.g., educational facilities, corporate workplaces, medical facilities, and prisons) combine to restrict social interaction or on the other hand promote open-ended social encounters while projecting the social power of institutions into public and private spheres of life. Freud's thought helps explain why the architect, and others, might have empathy for spaces of social encounter that separate, isolate, and formally configure social interactions. And Freud helps explain empathy for the opposite, as in the case of architect Rem Koolhaas' appreciation of undivided open areas intended to architecturally support emancipatory social interactions.

CHAPTER 2

Freud and modernity: selfhood and emancipatory self-determination

Freud first developed his system of thought in the historical context of the city of Vienna at the turn of the 20th century, a historical context often called *fin-de-siècle* Vienna. That time and place, widely regarded as a crucible of modernity, sets the stage for introducing Freud, his key ideas, and his clinical and cultural observations.

Freud was born into a Jewish family in 1856, in Freiberg, Moravia, close to Vienna. By present-day demographic benchmarks, Freud's family circumstances would be defined as low income, if not poor. Just before his 4th birthday, his family moved to Vienna, where he remained throughout his childhood, later earned his medical degree in 1881, and eventually opened his private practice in 1886 (Gay, 1989, xxxi).

Near the turn of the century, Freud developed an influential understanding of the structure of the human psyche and psychical experience and an understanding of relationships with special "objects," such as the mother's breast when nursing. Freud published important ideas on childhood trauma (1895), repression and screen memories (1899), dreams (1900), sexuality and the phases of development in childhood (1905 (1920)), lapses in speech and memory, e.g., "Freudian slips" (1901), and creative expression (1905, 1907, 1908b). The examples discussed in this chapter highlight important milestones in Freud's system of thought, their influence on the understanding of selfhood, and some of the implications for architecture studio culture today.

<u>Freud developed an influential understanding of the structure of the human psyche and psychical experience, and an understanding of relationships with special "objects"...</u>

Freud and Vienna: modernity and culture

At the turn of the 19th century, the early-modern interest in subjectivity and selfhood was reflected in the exploration of sexuality in the arts in Vienna and beyond Vienna in the exploration of empathy as a basis for aesthetic experience. *Fin-De-Siècle Vienna: Politics and Culture*, by Schorske, 1980, is an important and widely acknowledged study in the arts and humanities on the formation of political and cultural ideas in Vienna at the time. The defining features of modernity in Vienna then were, Schorske notes, a general "assimilation" to industrial practicality and profit motive, a cosmopolitan café-culture shared by professional and intellectual elites, "emancipation, opportunity," and a feeling of "uncertainty" associated with transformations and upheavals due to modernization (Schorske, 1980: xxvii, 63, 87, 119). In that historical frame, Schorske examines politics, arts, architecture, and Freud's *Interpretation of Dreams*, 1900. Vienna was a key site of experimentation in city development, including the Ringstrasse, which involved an unprecedented scale of new construction marked by contrasting style preferences. On the one hand, *fin-de-siècle* Vienna participated in "a kind of oedipal revolt" in the arts and architecture and the understanding of selfhood and self-determination. The revolt pitched the appreciation of subjective aspects of selfhood and self-determination against Austria's preexisting cultural emphasis on rational selfhood, self-discipline, and restraint. The revolt did not last long in the face of conservative reactionary counter-movements with Christian, nationalist, anti-Semitic, and socialist leanings (Schorske, 1980: xviii, 5).

At the turn of the 19th century, the early-modern interest in subjectivity and selfhood was reflected in the exploration of sexuality in the arts in Vienna and beyond Vienna in the exploration of empathy as a basis for aesthetic experience.

Contrasting architectural preferences in *fin-de-siècle* Vienna

Vienna, the city of Freud's *The Interpretation of Dreams*, 1900, was also the city of the architect and urban theorist Camillo Sitte, who wrote *City Building*, 1889, and architect and urban theorist Otto Wagner, who wrote *Modern Architecture*, 1895. By the turn of the century, Schorske explains, the Ringstrasse in Vienna, a circular swath of land between the inner city and outer city, had already undergone "beautification" developments in the Baroque style. At the center of the city stood the "The Fools Tower," a cylindrical building that had been purpose-built and functioned as an insane asylum from 1784 to 1886. Nearing the turn of the century, Camillo Sitte and Otto Wagner played leading but conflicting roles. Sitte and Wagner voiced passionate but contrasting concerns about architecture's response to modernity. Each was critical of developments in the Ringstrasse and held contrasting views on how to balance the new rational and functional demands of industrialization and modernity with social and psychological considerations. Sitte warned that the too-wide boulevards and other too-expansive open spaces of the Ringstrasse, all too-populated with vehicles, instilled alienation and the fear of open space, or rather a mental disorder called agoraphobia. The remedy, Sitte proposed, would be to build human-scaled buildings and public squares tailored to traditions of community life and to reduce the impact of vehicles. Wagner, on the other hand, sought to facilitate transportation and business and embraced the unprecedented modern scale of urban population densities in the city and along its periphery. He saw modern efficiency and technology as emancipating forces and viewed tradition as an obstacle to be overcome. The modern sensibility, indeed the modern psyche, Wagner believed, required architects to express functions and construction materials directly with little ornament (Schorske, 1980).

Vienna, the city of Freud's *The Interpretation of Dreams*, 1900, was also the city of the architect and urban theorist Camillo Sitte, who wrote *City Building*, 1889, and architect and urban theorist Otto Wagner, who wrote *Modern Architecture*, 1895.

Industrialization had already driven Gottfried Semper, theorist and architect, to a kind of architectural identity crisis. On the one hand, he designed the Neo-Renaissance style reconstruction of the Dresden Opera House, Germany, 1870–1878. On the other hand, he advanced the provocative idea that the exterior wall of modern architecture should be a technological shawl, a semitransparent "dressing" of steel and glass, wrapped around the otherwise naked structure of the building (Semper, 1860 (1989): 227, 254). Architecture style conflicts around this time arose amid general social concerns about the city as a metaphor of estrangement and locus of social anxiety, concerns represented in *The Metropolis and Mental Life*, 1903, by George Simmel, a German sociologist. Increasingly, social criticisms incorporated the medical terminology of neurosis and diagnosis such as agoraphobia (Vidler, 1994: 11–29).

Sitte and Wagner voiced passionate but contrasting concerns about architecture's response to modernity.

The Interpretation of Dreams, 1900

The large majority of the dreams Freud discusses in *The Interpretation of Dreams*, 1900, are dreams by others. Freud also self-analyzes a number of his dreams as well. Schorske links Freud's self-analysis with career frustrations up to that time, frustrations stemming from conservative as well as rationalist and anti-Semitic political movements. The highly unconventional new ideas that Freud espoused on unconscious drives, dream content, and sexuality positioned him in estranged and awkward circumstances relative to those in power who might otherwise have helped him rise professionally and socially. Nonetheless, Schorske notes, *The Interpretation of Dreams* offers an unprecedented view of human experience and a highly personal expression of Freud's idea that political behavior is a byproduct of psychical wishes. One of the central ideas of *The Interpretation of Dreams* is that the events of everyday life, including political events, rather profoundly shape dream content. At about the same time, Schorske notes that political barriers led the painter Gustav Klimt, whose sexuality explicit paintings put him at odds with reactionary political agendas, to begin a withdrawal into a private sphere of associations with little further social influence in Vienna (Schorske, 1980: 264).

Even in the view of reactionary politics of *fin-de-siècle* Vienna and elsewhere over time, the international emancipatory influence of Freud's system of thought on the understanding of human selfhood is widely acknowledged. Certainly, a lesson to be drawn from *fin-de-siècle* Vienna is that that modernity called into question longstanding social conventions and taboos and, by doing so, gave rise to reactionary politics clinging to restrictive notions of selfhood. One of the most pervasive systems of restriction on selfhood in Freud's lifetime stemmed from the Calvinist Reformed Church, widespread in Europe and North America. The church taught that the believer is a kind of spiritual priest, a notion of selfhood calling for self-control, abstinence, and traditional family values (Zaretsky, 2004: 39).

Staking out the structural psychical processes in childhood, Freud reasoned in *The Interpretation of Dreams*, 1900, that dreams express unconscious wishes. Selfhood, or rather the psychological make-up of the individual person, is shaped by developmental experiences in childhood, as Freud explained later in *Three Essays on the Theory of Sexuality* (1905 (1920)). Controversially, Freud describes the experiences as "sexual." What he means is that developmental experiences and behaviors such as breast-feeding and thumb-sucking in childhood are pleasurable and involve sensory organs that later in adulthood contribute to sexual experience. In that sense, childhood physical and psychological pleasures are precursors or "pregenital" forerunners to adulthood sexuality (Freud, 1905 (1920): 197–198). Among the many other key ideas, Freud presents in *Three Essays* the idea that the developmental experiences are universal, meaning that everyone passes through the same phases in childhood. Another idea is that the processes establish psychical dispositions, similar to character traits, dispositions that are expressed in adult dreams, thoughts, and behaviors. And Freud explained that the developmental phases, like unconscious wishes expressed in adult dreams, are defined in part by the child's relations with objects. Freud also suggested that these relations probably influence what the adult regards as "beautiful" (Freud, 1905 (1920): 156, 238).

<u>Aside from the reactionary politics of *fin-de-siècle* Vienna, the international emancipatory influence of Freud's system of thought on the understanding of human selfhood is widely acknowledged.</u>

Psychical selfhood and self-determination

Freud's ideas have been influential socially, partly because the ideas lend themselves to the interpretation of a wide range of key issues in modern popular culture: selfhood, desire, gender, family relations, group dynamics, and social phenomena including religion, democracy, fascism, racism, and violence. Freud applied his psychoanalytic ideas to bring the psychical dimensions of such issues into focus, thus encouraging wide-ranging applications of his ideas.

Freud's social influence is matched perhaps only by two other key figures in the 19th and 20th centuries: Karl Marx (1818–1883) and Henry Ford (1863–1947). Each introduced ideas with which to understand the new norms, practices, and other phenomena that define the shift from Victorian to modern life and modernity. Unlike Marx and Ford, Freud offered "the first great theory and practice of selfhood and 'personal life,'" and by doing so helped shape the norms and practices that came to define modernity (Zaretsky, 2004: 5). Yet Freud's theory and practice are highly controversial, with both praise and criticism from women's rights, philosophy, politics, literature, science, and psychoanalysis. One's appreciation of Freud's work must be tempered by substantive criticisms, outlined briefly here before moving on to aspects of Freud's work that stand on firmer ground.

Freud has been accused of being indifferent to science and of purposefully sidestepping criticisms regarding the scientific basis of his work (Coiffi, 1998: 115–116. Crews, 2017: 381). Freud's opinion seems to have waxed and waned on comparisons between psychoanalysis and science. Ultimately he suggested that insofar as psychoanalytic work is systematic, it is scientific. For example, psychoanalytic work involves "making plausible inferences and translating" to "fill in" "breaks in the sequence of 'psychical' events" (Freud, 1940: 158–159). Further, as a "scientific activity," psychoanalysis involves "describing phenomena and then proceeding to group, classify, and correlate them" (Freud, 1915a: 117).

Freud's female patients taught him a great deal clinically and theoretically, yet he maintained a stilted view of women, a view that is reflected in his published work. Peter Gay outlines the significant influence of female patients on Freud's clinical technique and theory, an influence that was only indirectly acknowledged by Freud (Gay, 1989: 78). Further, Eli Zaretsky, a historian and Freudian scholar, outlines Freud's gender bias in the "Dora" case, a case lasting for 3 months in 1900 involving a woman who was 18 years of age. Too simplistically, Freud summed up Dora's symptoms as hysteria due to a failure to resolve bisexual impulses. That diagnosis is now a notorious example of Freud's insensitivity to the social restrictions on women and the exploitation of women, which at the time were barriers to women's employment and the right to vote (Zaretsky, 2004; 55). Even more incriminatingly, Frederick Crews, an essayist and literary critic, highlights Freud's belittling interpretations of Dora's clinical musings, as well as patronizing attitudes expressed in Freud's engagement letters (*Brautbriefe)* to his fiancé Martha Berneys (Crews, 2017: 605–610, 46–48).

Partly due to those shortcomings, Freud's contributions to social emancipatory promises of modernity are, today, perhaps the least recognized and least appreciated aspects of Freud's influence. To better understand those contributions, it is helpful to consider three issue categories that have defined the emancipatory promises of modernity: selfhood and self-determination; sexuality and identity politics; nonexclusionary democracy and fascism. Zaretsky, and others indirectly, note that Freud's major writings established important ideas in support of those promises, even as the promises have evolved over time and place (Zaretsky, 2004: 111. Damousi and Plotkin, 2009: 4–8). The emphasis here shall be on Freud's thought about traumatic experience and his positive influence on the emancipatory promise of selfhood and self-determination.

The Interpretation of Dreams, 1900, illustrates how Freud's thought on personal life responded to social issues of his time. In that book, Freud explains how personal life and wishful dreams entwine with the events of daily life.

Trauma, repression, architecture of screen memories, remembering, repeating, and working through

Trauma disorders and traumatic experiences have come to be defined in terms of overwhelming feelings of helplessness in the face of threats to selfhood and self-identity. Threats to selfhood can take the form of physical threats and psychological threats. In the extreme case of combat trauma, informally called "shell shock," physical and psychological threats to selfhood are combined. Psychologically overwhelming negations of selfhood can be experienced in the face of entrapment in abusive situations, social isolation, exploitation, coercion, and captivity, any of which can lead to a disorienting loss of self-identity and selfhood. Raising awareness about traumatic experiences can be therapeutic and emancipatory for individuals as well as groups (Herman, 1992: 118. Zaretsky, 2015: 38–39).

Freud's influence on the understanding of traumatic experience bears in interesting ways on architecture studio culture and the social and psychological circumstances in which designs are produced. The modern architect and architecture students have direct experience with architecture studio culture and the demands of design studio projects. Notoriously, architecture studio projects involve prolonged periods of self-criticism and critique by others where one's control of the project and one's views are constantly in question. Typically, accolades are long withheld, if ever fully granted – after all, a design is never complete. Forgoing other commitments, one could always make a few more studies to improve this or that aspect of a design. Design studio also often involves sleep-deprived days of toil and fatigue and poor diet before deadlines and presentations. Presentations are usually made for a number of critics or "jurors." Standing before critics, student presenters may struggle with "stage fright" and the delirium of insomnia to maintain orderly thought. And, in the face of criticism when a presenter's efforts and "gifts" are questioned, feelings of helplessness and situational detachment can arise, signaled by a "thousand-yard stare." Repeated experiences such as these can bring about feelings of shame and disorienting challenges to selfhood. Indeed, transformation of character from neophyte to architect is the objective of professional training. Recent US National Architecture Accreditation Board (NAAB) concerns about architecture studio culture and student well-being (*2014 Conditions for Accreditation*) bring into focus the need to better understand threats to selfhood in studio settings. Freud's influence on the understanding of trauma helps illuminate the psychical dimensions of such issues.

Freud's influence on the understanding of traumatic experience bears in interesting ways on architecture studio culture and the social and psychological circumstances in which designs are produced.

In *Studies on Hysteria*, 1895, Freud outlines his thought at the time on debilitating psychological disorders, thought important to understanding shell-shock disorders in WWI and after. *Studies on Hysteria* was written by Freud and Josef Breuer, who was one of Freud's primary colleagues at the time. The book was an outgrowth of Freud's training under Jean-Martin Charcot (1825–1893), as well as Freud's and Breuer's clinical practices prior to 1895. Charcot was a highly influential neurologist at the Salpêtrière hospital in Paris, where Freud trained in 1885. Famously, Charcot presented some of his patients, mostly women, in public "theater," demonstrating the expressions of "hysteria," including trance-like physical behavior, paralysis, delirium, and fainting disorders. Charcot's theater is rather famously depicted in the painting "A Clinical Lesson at the Salpêtrière" by Pierre Aristide André, Brouillet, 1887. Even before Charcot, hysteria had been clinically diagnosed and documented, and by the second half of the 19th century it was widely regarded as a particular kind of neurosis. Neurosis, a term Charcot and Freud adopted, was a catch-all term coined much earlier by William Cullen in 1769 (Piñero, 1989: 1). By Charcot's time, the term neurosis had come to represent a wide range of disorders such as nervous exhaustion, the clinical term for which was "neurasthenia" (Beard 1869: 741). Neurosis disorders were thought to be signs of an overtaxed or perhaps overly sensitive nervous system, conditions that Charcot and his predecessors thought to be symptomatic of hereditary weaknesses.

A strange grouping of other behaviors such as fear of open space, wandering, dreaminess, theatricality, and homosexuality was also counted as symptoms of neuroses at the time. The general idea was that the technological phenomena of modernity could overtax the human nervous system. Some examples of overwhelming phenomena were industrialization, trains, and demolition of parts of the city. Adding to the issues was the massive scale of some new construction for homogeneous urban beautification and infrastructure projects, most prominently in Vienna and Paris. In Paris, the urban planner Georges-Eugène Haussmann built a network of new boulevards, demolishing swaths of historic neighborhoods. In popular culture at the time, neuroses came to be viewed as a social problem, a sign of the dehumanizing aspects of modernization, leading increasingly to estrangement. Sitte, 1889, as explained above, was a leading proponent of that view. Before Sitte, the intellectual Charles Baudelaire also gave voice to such estrangements in "Parisian Scenes," 1861, *The Flowers of Evil*. In Baudelaire's Paris, the Salpêtrière, where Freud worked with Charcot for a short time, functioned as a kind of hospice and detention facility for vagrants, prostitutes, and those with symptoms of hysteria. The Salpêtrière building and its inhabitants personified Baudelaire's estranged anti-heroes of modernity.

In Paris, the urban planner Georges-Eugène Haussmann built a network of new boulevards, demolishing swaths of historic neighborhoods. In popular culture at the time, neuroses came to be viewed as a social problem, a sign of the dehumanizing aspects of modernization, leading increasingly to estrangement.

Not long after, in the last quarter of the 19th century, Charcot presented patients in theater at the Salpêtrière to demonstrate symptoms of hysteria and hypnotic techniques used to treat patients. Initially a disciple of Charcot, Freud came to believe, with Breuer and some others, in the psychological basis of hysteria rather than the hereditary basis. Later, Freud reluctantly abandoned hypnosis as a form of treatment. Pierre Janet in France, in *L'automatisme psychologique*, 1889, and then Freud and Breuer in *Studies on Hysteria*, 1895, suggested that hysteria is a result of internal psychological defenses enlisted to fend off excessive stimulation associated with traumatic experiences. Internal defenses split the conscious into that which can be integrated into consciousness versus traumatic experiences that could not be integrated, the later producing trance-like dissociative behaviors characteristic of hysteria.

Studies on Hysteria established the clinical and theoretical context for an analytical diagram that Freud drew by hand earlier in 1897 in a letter to a colleague Wilhelm Fliess, a letter that Freud titled "The Architecture of Hysteria" (Freud, 1897: 251). The diagram has been redrawn here in Figure 1. The diagram depicts memory-scenes, similar to scenes that dreams are made of, at various depths of repression. It indicates how patients with debilitating symptoms of a traumatic experience in childhood have buried the memory of the traumatic

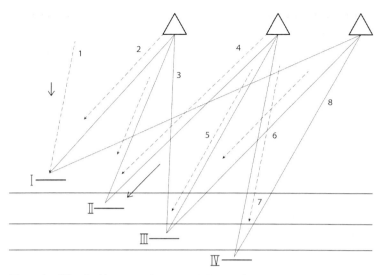

Figure 1 "The Architecture of Hysteria," Sigmund Freud, 1897, redrawn: memory-scenes and depth of repression. Triangles represent "Symptoms" e.g., memory scenes, phantasies. Dashed lines, arrows, and numbers represent the paths of psychoanalytic "Work" uncovering the connections (solid lines) between symptoms and depths of repression I, II, III, IV.

experience by repressing the memories. That is to say, disturbing memory-scenes are put down and covered over by much less troubling memories, distancing the troubling memory from conscious thought.

"The Architecture of Hysteria"…diagram depicts memory-scenes, similar to scenes that dreams are made of, at various depths of repression…

Freud added to this line of reasoning in "Childhood Memories and Screen Memories" in *The Psychopathology of Everyday Life*, 1901. There, he explains that repressed memory-scenes are hidden behind "screen memories." A repressed scene is displaced by means of "association" and "substitution" with less troubling memories. A screen memory results from substitution and "displacement" of a hidden and more troubling memory. The screen memory masks the more troubling memory but cannot do away with it. That way, the screen memory covers over the repressed memory of a traumatic event. Freud says a screen memory can be recalled more or less "indifferently" and so more readily diverts attention from the memory of the original trauma. Nonetheless, a screen memory owes its existence and significance to the repressed original scene. Similarly, dream images and "slips of the tongue" can represent associations, substitutions, displacements, as well as "condensations" of memory content that give rise to a screen memories (Freud, 1901: 58–59). A dream image represents psychical experience in a very condensed way often by associating a number of insignificant image associations, word associations, thought associations, or any combination of those associations (Freud, 1900: 281–282). Condensation, displacement, substitution, screen memory, and repression are the key elements of the "Architecture of Hysteria," altogether explaining the unconscious processes of psychical representation. With those concepts, Freud's theory of psychical representation explains how dream images, slips of the tongue, screen memories, thought connections, fantasies, actions, and objects in the external world acquire psychical double meanings.

A shared feature of the examples, Freud says, is a seemingly insignificant detail at the center of a scene that defines the screen memory, an insignificant tangential detail of a troubling original scene. The insignificant detail is substituted for the troubling details of the traumatic scene. The traumatic details lay "hidden" and "forgotten" behind an otherwise insignificant though persistent screen memory. Unconsciously, the patient avoids the memory of a traumatic event by favoring "one memory while striving to work against another" (Freud, 1901: 43, 45).

Memory scenes and their connections can be uncovered in clinical work while talking with the patient. Clinical "work," Freud explains, involves uncovering the connections and calling a patient's attention to them, an awareness-raising activity that eventually dissolves the debilitating symptoms of trauma, symptoms that stem from the original traumatic experience (Freud, 1897: 251). In *Remembering, Repeating, and Working Through*, 1914, Freud elaborated on the clinical technique for helping patients overcome repressed traumatic experiences that might be at the bottom of neurotic behaviors. The technique is now widely known as "the talking cure," a phrase attributed to a patient "Anna O," whose case history is presented in *Studies on Hysteria*. By talking with the patient, or rather by getting the patient to talk without self-censoring, particularly encouraging the patient to freely associate, memories as well as resistance to memories can be identified. Psychical representations in the form of dream images, slips of the tongue, screen memories, thought connections, phantasies, objects in the external world, and actions are examined (Freud, 1914: 148–150). For example, in the clinical setting, screen memories are signs of unconscious resistance to remembering a trauma, signs of repression. Psychotherapy involves overcoming resistance to remembering. By bringing the traumatic memory into consciousness, the traumatic memory can be consciously affirmed. And, given voice in the relatively safe clinical setting, the memory can be consciously reprocessed and gradually worked through. Thus, by "remembering, repeating, and working through" memories of traumatic experiences, disabling symptoms can be overcome (Freud, 1914: 155–156)

Shell shock, also widely known as combat trauma, is a compelling example of an adult life-world phenomenon leading Freud to refine his theory of neuroses as well as his theory of the psyche. Prior to WWI, for example in *The Psychopathology of Everyday Life*, Freud explained that a troubling memory linked to childhood can break through into adult conscious thought by associations in the everyday life-world. Thus, the original traumatic experience can have a deferred effect and lead to debilitating symptoms. Freud recognized that shell shock was a trauma that originated in adulthood, not childhood. Shell shock was a more or less immediate consequence of an overwhelming external-world event in the adult life-world. Shell shock symptoms arose as effects of overwhelming traumatic threats in combat. Freud reasoned that, in normal circumstances, anxiety is experienced as a prompt to somehow avoid threats that might render one helpless. Unavoidable and overpowering combat experiences overpower the normal ability to avoid threats to selfhood, leaving the soldier traumatized. Dazed or trance-like behaviors are among the symptoms of combat trauma, often epitomized by the characteristic "thousand-yard stare" of combat trauma victims.

Freud's thoughts on hysteria contributed to the treatment of WWI soldiers overwhelmed by shell shock. At first, misunderstood and disparaged, soldiers with shell shock gradually came to be viewed by many as having a psychological wound, although WWI shell shock victims were mainly persecuted as unmanly, weak, and disobedient (Zaretsky, 2004: 121). By the time of WWII, combat trauma was recognized as an inevitable psychological consequence of war and regarded as a problem that could be treated. Treatment involved limiting a soldier's combat exposure and recognizing the emotional codependency of soldiers in a combat unit. After the Vietnam War, the US Veteran's Administration funded a lengthy report on "post-traumatic stress disorder," acknowledging combat trauma as a legacy of the war. By 1980, post-traumatic stress disorder was listed in the American Psychiatric Association's *Diagnostic and Statistical Manual of Mental Disorders, Third Edition (DSM-III)* as a diagnostic category of mental disorder. More recently, *DSM-IV*, 2000, includes generalized anxiety disorder as a category of mental disorder with less extreme symptoms, not involving actual or threatened physical violence as in post-traumatic stress disorder. Generalized anxiety disorder, as a diagnostic category, recognizes culture, age, and gender variations in the physical and mental expression of an anxiety disorder (*DSM-IV*, 2000: 472–475).

<u>By the time of WWII, combat trauma was recognized as an inevitable psychological consequence of war and regarded as a problem that could be treated. Treatment involved limiting a soldier's combat exposure and recognizing the emotional codependency of soldiers in a combat unit.</u>

Among the most important of Freud's observations on trauma, and on shell shock as a specific kind of trauma, is the inability to avoid a potential threat and helplessness in the face of threat. In other words, an overwhelming threat is a threat to selfhood, and the inability to avoid the threat is a violation of self-determination. Adult experiences of "psychical helplessness," Freud wrote in "Anxiety and Instinctual Life," hark back to troubling experiences in childhood when, for example, an infant is faced with the potential loss of its primary objects "or loss of love" (Freud, 1933: 88). All of Freud's foundational ideas outlined above on trauma and on remembering, repeating, and working through trauma are reaffirmed by Judith Herman, a clinical psychiatrist, in *Trauma and Recovery*, 1992. Herman identifies categories of experience in which trauma often occurs: disconnection, captivity, domestic abuse and exploitation, sexual abuse and rape, child abuse, and terror. Helplessness figures prominently in each. Further, the conscious affirmation of traumatic experience, which can include group-affirmation and group "consciousness-raising," is considered central to recovery from traumatic experiences (Herman, 1992).

Cultural screens, disconnection, negation, and affirmation

Disconnection experience is quite relevant to concerns in the United States for the mental health of architecture students, concerns expressed by the American Institute of Architecture Students (AIAS) in *The Redesign of Studio Culture*, 2002, and reiterated in the *2014 NAAB Conditions for Accreditation*. Herman explains, in trauma, disconnection is experienced as a "shattering...of the self that is formed and sustained in relations to others." Disconnection arises from a break in the "attachments of family, friendship, love, and community," attachments that reinforce one's belief system. Disconnection leaves one in a state of "existential crisis," estranged, feeling that one's own opinion and needs do not count, questioning one's value, and feeling shameful (Herman, 1997, 51–52). Traumatic disconnection reopens and violates the ways childhood development struggles for "autonomy, initiative, competence, identity, and intimacy" were resolved (Herman, 1997, 52). In such cases, victim behavior can swing from withdrawal and self-isolation to clinging to others. The effect of disturbing events hinges somewhat on the vulnerability of the person in question. For example, WWII studies report that some soldiers "broke" more readily than others (Pols and Oak, 2007: 12).

While trauma and post-traumatic stress disorder are usually linked to rather extreme events, as in the cases of combat experience, sexual abuse, and terrorism, disconnection is certainly generally relevant to less extreme events, experiences, and extreme generalized anxiety disorder. Trauma theory has been applied recently to identify and affirm the anxiety experienced by large population groups when faced with external threats to selfhood and self-determination. Black, Latino, Muslim, and LGBT communities in the United States have experienced high levels of anxiety and tension due to sustained and unavoidable discriminatory rhetoric and the "abuse, torture, and exclusion an individual suffers solely due to their identity and circumstances" (Bramble, 2019). The anxiety can trigger difficult unconscious associations interfering with normal functioning in the adult life-world. When unavoidable, an overwhelming threat surpasses anxiety as a signal for avoidance behavior and can lead to the disabling symptoms of trauma.

…trauma-theory has been applied recently to identify and affirm the anxiety experienced by large population groups when faced with external threats to selfhood and self-determination.

Freud's understanding of traumatic experience, and subsequent developments building on that foundation, add theoretical support to concerns about design studio culture and architecture students' health. The specific concerns of the AIAS and NAAB are that modern architecture studio culture promotes and perpetuates myths that negatively influence student experience and student behavior. Many of the myths listed in the AIAS report perpetuate experiences that are characteristic of the traumatic experiences that have been identified with post-traumatic stress disorder. For example, there is the myth that "[t]he creation of architecture should be a solo, artistic struggle." (Koch, 2002, 6). That is to say, studio culture isolates the student by expecting the student to work alone on a design in the studio next to other students who are expected to work "solo." Further, there is the stipulation that "[s]tudents should not have a life outside of architecture school" (Koch, 2002, 6). In other words, the student, already working alone in studio, is also expected to disconnect from and abandon his or her family, friends, love interests, and community. In another example, "[s]tudents must devote themselves to studio in order to belong to the architecture community" (Koch, 2002, 6). That is to say, the "love" of the architecture community (peers, faculty, and professionals) will be withheld from the student who does not demonstrate devotion to design studio. Further still is the myth that "[i]t is more important to finish a few extra drawings than to sleep or mentally prepare for the design review" (Koch, 2002, 6). This myth suggests 3 kinds of experience that could be traumatizing for the student. First, sleep deprivation is widely regarded as a torture technique that leads to behavioral impairments similar to trauma symptoms. Second, sleep deprivation symptoms such as fatigue, disordering of thought, and delirium could give rise to the student experiencing a loss of personal character, particularly if sleep deprivation is frequent. And third, the sleep-deprived presenter could feel shame and public humiliation with the loss of the "normal self" in front of critics and peers during presentation. In the final example, there is the myth that "[s]tudents do not have the power to make changes within architecture programs or the design studio" (Koch, 2002, 6). In other words, student's self-determination is negated by an inability to avoid the repetition of traumatic experiences associated with sleep deprivation, fatigue, disordering of thought, delirium, loss of personal character, and shame.

The myths examined here are codes of conduct for studio performance, although they are not described as such in any professional practice guidelines or university studio syllabi. As with any system of rules for social and professional conduct, nonconformance is taboo, and non-conformers are weaned from the system. The implications for enrollment in architecture programs, for entering into the profession, and for a lasting career as an architect are significant. Certainly, as Schorske explained in *Fin-De-Siècle Vienna*, provoking longstanding cultural taboos can give rise to reactionary politics. Such issues weigh on the well-being of the architecture student and the professional architect. Remembering, repeating, and working through the issues could be emancipatory and could support selfhood and self-determination.

The affirmation of traumatic experience has been helpful and emancipatory in various cultural contexts (Herman, 1992. Zaretsky, 2009. Lee, 2019). Zaretsky offers a poignant example, calling attention to Freud's influence on consciousness-raising in African-American literature dealing with historical and unconscious memories of racism and cultural taboos. The term "racial unconscious" arose at the intersection of African-American intellectual thought and psychoanalytic theory at the time of the Harlem Renaissance in the 1920s. A racial unconscious signified a collective unconscious that shared a cultural and historic legacy, affirming black selfhood and self-determination. Later, the African-American writer, Richard Wright, drew from Freud's thought on repression and screen memory for literary inspiration exploring psychical-cultural screens of racism that configure relations between perpetrator and victim. In Wright's characters, screens unconsciously serve to mask race issues that lay buried behind the screens, screens that cover rage and shame, mask disturbing unconscious associations to "primitive" culture and "high" culture, male and bisexual and female, sensuality and abstinence, cultural belonging, and cultural homelessness. Over time, historically and culturally layered screen memories of racism in the collective and individual racial unconscious become signs pointing to negations of race, negations of self, and negations by exclusion. In these ways, and in many others, Freud's thought on trauma supported the emancipatory promises of modernity by affirming subjective dimensions of selfhood and self-determination, sexuality and identity, as well as non-exclusionary democracy, racism, and fascism (Zaretsky, 2004: 110, 143–156. Zaretsky, 2009: 6, 46–58).

Conclusion

To summarize, Freud began developing his understanding of trauma, the unconscious, dreams, sexuality, and psychical aspects of everyday life in the historical context of *fin-de-siècle* Vienna. By the time Sitte, Wagner, and Freud started to publish their ideas near the turn of the century, sexually inflected notions of selfhood, architecture, city streets, cafés, and shopping arcades had become part of the fabric of modern experience.

By linking psychical processes shared by all to the individual subjective experiences of everyday life, Freud also offered influential psychological perspectives on the emancipatory promises of modernity. In this chapter, the emphasis has been on emancipatory promises regarding selfhood and self-determination.

Freud is widely credited for the modern emancipatory understanding of sexuality, identity, the unconscious, trauma, repression, and therapeutic techniques involving remembering, repeating, and working through trauma. Freud's diagram of memory-scenes and layers of repression sums up how screen memories mask and resist the memory of traumatic experience. These ideas have long functioned as tools to think with and to analyze social and cultural phenomena. Trauma theory tools were applied in this chapter to explore architecture studio culture myths and taboos and the potentially traumatic experience of them.

CHAPTER 3

Aesthetic experience: the object, empathy, the unconscious, and architectural design

Architecture theorists and designers have sought to understand the aesthetic experience, how people unconsciously experience and identify with architectural objects, and why certain kinds of design, or design forms, might be more satisfying than others. The particular focus has been on the experience of architectural environments and the formal characteristics of architectural objects. For example, as outlined in Chapter 1, Rowe and Slutsky explored literal and phenomenal transparency of modern building façades as the basis for aesthetic experience. And earlier, as outlined in Chapter 2, Semper, Sitte, and Wagner separately explored architectural enclosure and open-ended space relations.. Similarly, in *Prolegomena for a Psychology of Architecture*, 1886, Heinrich Wölfflin sought to explain why "closed form" might be pleasing. Based on the idea that the human body is a closed form, Wölfflin concluded that, aesthetically, closed form is ideal and best for architecture. Later, in 1928, Siegfried Giedion, the noted modern architecture historian, proposed that modern architecture "unconsciously…strives to overcome the old… fortress-like incarceration." In contrast with Wölfflin, Giedion advocated spatial "interplay with the city," "floating relations and interpenetrations" whereby "[t]he boundaries of architecture are blurred" such that distinctions between the individual, building, site, and city are minimal (Giedion, 1928: 87, 147). However, Giedion did not explain how or why the unconscious might strive in one or another way toward blurred boundaries.

Architecture theorists and designers have sought to understand aesthetic experience, how people unconsciously experience

and identify with architectural objects, and why certain kinds of design, or design forms, might be more satisfying than others.

Giedion, like Wölfflin, Wagner, and Sitte separately sought to explain aesthetic experience in architecture without actually explaining the psychological basis for it. In other words, they alluded to but did not actually explain the psychological basis of preferences for or against closed form or, on the other hand, open form and interpenetrating space relations. Freud's system of thought helps explain how a person unconsciously identifies with objects, and why one architect or theorist might advance ideas about aesthetic intuition that contrast with the ideas of another. To understand how Freud can help explain these issues, it is useful to first look more closely into how aesthetic intuition has been explained, both before Freud and then after. Hence, this chapter stakes out a cross-section of architectural thought on aesthetic experience, beginning with Gottfried Semper, 1851, before Freud and *fin-de-siècle* Vienna, 1900, ending with representative examples of more recent architects and theorists who have drawn from psychoanalytic theory to explain aesthetic intuition, how people unconsciously experience and identify with architecture, and what leads to pleasing or displeasing experience. The special focus shared by almost all is on psychological motivations that might influence the aesthetic intuition of architecture and the formal characteristics of architectural objects that might contribute to aesthetic experience.

Unconsciously projecting oneself and intuiting the shape or form of an art object: Semper, Vischer, Schmarsow, Wölfflin, Giedion, and Moholy-Nagy

Gottfried Semper (1803–1879) is an important reference in the architectural understanding of aesthetic intuition. He shifted the traditional emphasis in architectural aesthetics from outward form as an expression of a type of architectural ideal to form as an expression of internal primal human motives projected outward. Semper coined the phrase "principle of dressing" to explain what he believed to be the main motive that is outwardly projected to make architecture. Semper explained that the principle of dressing is a spatial motive, that is to say, it is a motive that seeks to tailor varying degrees of enclosure to satisfy needs for gathering and needs for symbolic communication (Semper, 1860 (1989): 227, 254). This reasoning led Semper to the idea that the exterior wall of a modern building need not appear to be load-bearing, as in traditional architecture. Rather, people intuitively understand the principle of dressing and that a wall is really just a kind of dressing, and, like clothing draped over their body, a wall can hang from a structural frame to provide enclosure. Also, like clothing, the wall can represent what is enclosed. Thus, Semper's principle of dressing implicitly advanced the idea that aesthetic intuition projects internal motives outward, the idea that internal motives drive the creative production of architecture, and the idea that internal motives shape the aesthetic experience of architecture. Questions concerning the psychological dimensions of internal motives were taken up by "empathy theorists" soon after Semper introduced the principle of dressing.

The writings of Vischer, Schmarsow, and Wölfflin in the latter part of the 19th century represent a sea change in the understanding of aesthetic intuition, culminating in what is now called empathy theory (Mallgrave and Ikonomou, 1994: 4–5). Empathy theorists explored the human ability to identify with objects by intuitively projecting internal preferences and states of mind and perhaps moods onto objects.

Empathy theorists explored the human ability to identify with objects by intuitively projecting internal preferences and states of mind and perhaps moods onto objects.

Robert Vischer in "On the Optical Sense of Form," 1873, is a key point of reference because – though he preceded Freud – Vischer's ideas on aesthetic intuition agree rather well with Freud's thought on human relations with objects, particularly how the psyche is projected in relations with objects. Vischer put forward the idea that aesthetic empathy hinges on the human capacity to "unconsciously" wrap oneself in the contours of an object "as in a garment." That notion of intuitively projecting oneself so as to envelope oneself with the shape or form of an art object is quite like Semper's principle of dressing. Vischer would certainly have been familiar with Semper's principle of dressing. However, Vischer explains, inspiration for his idea of empathy was *The Life of the Dream*, by Karl Scherner, 1861. Vischer writes that Scherner revealed to him the idea that through dreams a human "unconsciously projects its own bodily form – and with this the soul – into the form of the object. From this, I derived the notion that I call 'empathy'" (Vischer, 1873: 92). Aesthetic intuition, as in dreams, facilitates "pure absorption in which we imagine this or that phenomenon in accordance with the unconscious need for a surrogate for our body ego" (Vischer, 1873: 101) Uniquely, Vischer linked the notion of aesthetic identification with objects to the unconscious and intuitive outward projection of the self, to intuitively envelope oneself in the contours of the object as if the contours were the threads of a shroud. With Vischer's understanding of aesthetic intuition and imagination, human body form can be secondary, a cloud can be a surrogate for the body, and one can imagine oneself to be a cloud. Imagination facilitates a "hybrid" of sensations and wishful imaginings and the substitutions of the self-image for that of an external object (Vischer, 1873: 101–102). That is to say, imaginatively and intuitively, if not unconsciously, the body ego can transform into a cloud ego and the aesthetic experience of that can be pleasing. This set of ideational connections is more compelling because later, in *The Interpretation of Dreams*, 1900, Freud described Scherner's observations on dreams and the unconscious as being quite helpful and generally in agreement with his own (Freud, 1900: 83).

August Schmarsow, in "The Essence of Architectural Creation," 1893, asserts the principle of architectural "space creation." Space creation warrants mention here because it closely relates to Semper's notion of space as something that is configured by innate motives for enveloping and enclosing (the principle of dressing). However, Schmarsow's principle of space creation emphasizes interior space more than the enveloping wall. Architecture "creates, in a way no other art can, enclosures for us." Interior space is the ideal "emanation of the human being present" – a key aspect of architecture enabling it to function as the "place of the subject." Further, for Schmarsow, space creation does more than simply establish a place for a person or a social group, it creates space that becomes a surrogate or substitute for them. Thus, space "can take the place of the original subject" or social group, as suggested by the space of a courthouse, a sacred space, or great hall of a school (Schmarsow, 1893: 286, 289, 292). Unlike Semper, Schmarsow underscored literal correspondences between physical body, sensory experiences linked to the body, and space creation architecture (Schmarsow, 1893: 286, 289, 292). The physiological orientation of Schmarsow's ideas reflects the physician and philosopher Wilhelm Wundt's research on the physiological basis of aesthetic intuition in *Principles of Physiological Psychology*, 1874, quite influential among empathy theorists (Mallgrave and Ikonomou, 1994: 15, 58).

...for Schmarsow, space creation does more than simply establish a place for a person or a social group, it creates space that becomes a surrogate or substitute for them. Thus, space "can take the place of the original subject" or social group...

Heinrich Wölfflin's *Prolegomena to a Psychology of Architecture*, 1886, and *Principles of Art History*, 1915, are important points of reference in the history of empathy theory, not least because some of his premises go unquestioned even today. In contrast with Vischer, Wölfflin subscribed almost wholeheartedly to the idea that the psychological enjoyment of aesthetic objects, and the intuitive experience of objects, hinges rather literally on physiological sensations identified with the body. Thus, Wölfflin's ideas about aesthetic experience are, he wrote, based on the "time-honored" correspondences between the body and architecture. "Physical forms possess a character only because we ourselves possess a body...with a body...we gather the experience that enables us to identify with other forms" (Wölfflin, 1886: 151). And, "[o]ur own bodily organization is the form through which we apprehend everything physical" (Wölfflin, 1886: 157–158). This agrees with Wundt's view on physiological basis of aesthetic intuition (*Principles of Physiological Psychology,* 1874), and Wölfflin invites the comparison (Wölfflin, 1886: 158, 165). Wölfflin emphasizes "general laws of form," and the physical "limitation in space" figures prominently, taken literally in the sense that "individuality" hinges on "demarcation" from context and where supporting laws such as regularity, symmetry, and proportion are, thus, linked to human temperament (Wölfflin, 1886: 162). Hence, form becomes an "image of our own physical existence" and "will." Beyond this, Wölfflin introduces the idea that "matter…aspires toward form," and "longs for form" (Wölfflin, 1886: 160), a nod to the philosopher Arthur Schopenhauer's *The World as Will and Representation,* 1818–1819. There, Schopenhauer proposed the idea that, ultimately, human experience is best understood as a representation of the human will to life, e.g., striving and desire. Without self-restraint, he advised, striving and desire lead to ruin. Thus, Wölfflin suggests the will to form contrasts with "formlessness" as "basic conditions of organic life." The formless is "heavyhearted, depressed," a "physical disturbance" (Wölfflin, 1886: 160). That is to say, for Wölfflin, closed form and symmetry are ideal, and formlessness and open-ended space relations are not. Implicitly, by linking will to form and human temperament with laws that bound architectural form, Wölfflin hinted that the best architecture represents human will to form and the restraint of will to form. The implication is that one can aesthetically intuit the expression of striving and restraint in contours of an architectural object and find that pleasing. Later, in *Principles of Art History*, 1915, at a loss to explain the pervasiveness of a kind of will to formlessness in architecture, except, perhaps, negatively as an expression of inevitable the cycle of life, Wölfflin would reluctantly acknowledge it as a category of expression defined as "open form" (Wölfflin, 1915: 15).

In *Building in France, Building in Iron, Building in Ferroconcrete*, 1928, Sigfried Giedion describes examples of modern architecture in France as "emanations of the highest impulse: LIFE! To grasp life as a totality, to allow no divisions" (Giedion, 1928: 87). *Building in France* is an important milestone in the architectural understanding of aesthetic intuition because Giedion, unlike his former teacher Wölfflin, praises architecture that expresses a will to formlessness. And what had already become a wide-spread architectural fascination with open-form-and-space-relations is personified in Giedion's rousing account of a massive ferry transporter. The photograph of the transporter in *Building in France* reveals that the transporter is an open web steel trussed structure. As mentioned earlier, Giedion explains that the transporter is an example of "new architecture" that "unconsciously...strives to overcome the old...fortress-like incarceration" and exhibits spatial "interplay with the city," "floating relations and interpenetrations" liberating architecture and the city from the oppressive laws of closed form (Giedion, 1928: 87).

Certainly, Vischer, Schmarsow, Wölfflin, and Giedion put forward compelling but very different ideas about the psychology of aesthetic intuition, that people unconsciously identify with aesthetic objects, and what leads to pleasing or displeasing experience. The contrast between Vischer and Wölfflin is striking. Vischer draws his understanding of the unconscious from the logic of dreams; body form is secondary. Wölfflin bases his understanding of psychology on organic striving; body form is primary. However, for both Vischer and Wölfflin, aesthetic intuition involves the psychological projection of a self-image where the object becomes a representation of the self. The contrast between Wölfflin and his former student Giedion is also striking. Wölfflin idealizes the aesthetic virtues of closed form and denigrates open form. Giedion idealizes open form and eschews closed form. Wölfflin and Giedion base their understanding of aesthetic intuition on unconscious longing or striving, for form on the one hand (Wölfflin) and on the other hand for formlessness (Giedion).

László Moholy-Nagy, an influential artist and Bauhaus teacher who provided the graphic design and typesetting for Giedion's book *Building in France*, explored questions on the psychology of aesthetic intuition in his own book, *The New Vision*, 1928. Whereas Giedion's book emphasizes the analysis of existing objects such as the ferry transporter, in *The New Vision*, Moholy-Nagy emphasizes design practice as a basis for exploring aesthetic intuition.

Perhaps because Moholy-Nagy was an artist, he crossed a threshold that empathy theorists before him had not crossed. Where Schmarsow described architecture as a "space creation" phenomenon, Moholy-Nagy used drawing as a means to explore his own intuition of "space relations." That is to say, he sought to articulate "the quality of space creation itself...the actual felt quality of spatial creation." Moholy-Nagy's description calls attention to the idea that design drawing can be a basis for exploring aesthetic intuition and can be employed instrumentally, systematically, and strategically to explore aesthetic intuition. Moreover, Moholy-Nagy's description communicates his preference for open-form "space relations" as opposed to closed form. In *The New Vision*, Moholy-Nagy describes space creation as a matter of the "interweaving of the parts of space...a fluctuating play of forces...the nexus of spatial entities" (Moholy-Nagy, 1928: 59–64). In these ways, Moholy-Nagy signposts the formal opening up of designerly thoughts and activities as vehicles for the architectural investigation of spatial intuition and empathy. This opening is not marked by an art-historical description of effects, rather it is marked by projective acts of design and by the reflective contemplation on what creative work reveals about unconscious preferences. While Moholy-Nagy's studies were intentionally introspective, attempting to draw out unconscious feelings for architectural form, *The New Vision* only hints at the psychoanalytic meaning of such designerly thoughts and activities. Even though explicit references to psychoanalysis had already begun to appear at that time in Surrealist art, explicit architectural attempts to generate designs based on psychoanalytic concepts would come later with Richard Neutra, after Adrian Stokes.

Perhaps because Moholy-Nagy was an artist, he...used drawing as a means to explore his own intuition of "space relations."

Stone and phantasy, smooth and rough

Adrian Stokes (1902–1972) and his book *Stones of Rimini*, 1934, are important references for psychoanalytically informed interpretations of art and architecture, particularly concerning the Italian Renaissance. In *Stones of Rimini*, Stokes detects psychological "fantasies connected with material (always in the last resort, stone)…directly and emphatically expressed" (Stokes, 1934: 25). Stokes based that idea on the work of Freudian psychoanalyst Melanie Klein (1882–1960) and her notion of psychological reparation. Further, Stokes theorized that the architecture of the Italian Renaissance expresses universal psychical positions, the "manic" and the "depressive," positions that Klein found to be expressed in infant phantasies (the psychoanalytic term for fantasy). The positions arise as a normal course of events in the gradual separation from the mother in infancy and gradual acceptance that the mother is not simply an extension of "self" but rather is a separate whole being. In infancy, the separation is accompanied by feelings of loss and conflicting feelings about the loss. The manic position is characterized by spite; the depressive position is reparative. On the one hand, the loss is experienced as a loss of a part of the self, and in the same sense, the mother is experienced as somehow incomplete or unsatisfactory. Klein believed the loss, spiteful emotions, and need for reparation are reflected in children's play and creativity, particularly highly imaginative play "phantasies" that blur distinctions between play objects and mother. The earliest phantasies in infancy, Klein noted, are associated with separation from the mother and the infant's experience of separation as the loss of an object. Very early on for the infant, the object is not experienced so much as "mother" but rather as "me," as if the object was part of itself, suggesting a kind of blissful but provisional narcissism. Gradually, the breast "behaves" as if it were "defiant" and something other than "me." This leads to spiteful frustrations with the object and gradually with the mother represented as "defiant" objects. The frustrations are represented in phantasies, phantasies in which the object is "punished" for disobedience and phantasies in which the punished object can "retaliate." Spiteful phantasies, Klein noted, are symptomatic of the "manic position." Play can also express a wish for reparation, which is associated with the depressive position, which gradually involves restoring "love" for the mother and the self as separate beings, and resolving guilt associated with spiteful phantasies (Klein, 1929: 212–218. Klein, 1935: 262). In adulthood, art can be experienced unconsciously as "reparative" and, thus, can lead to a "satisfactory" aesthetic experience. That is to say, a satisfying aesthetic experience can arise from objects that offer the possibility to unconsciously affirm the need for reparation (Segal, 1952: 196–207).

Freudian psychoanalyst Melanie Klein (1882–1960)…believed … loss, spiteful emotions, and need for reparation are reflected in children's play and creativity, particularly, highly imaginative play "phantasies" that blur distinctions between play objects and mother.

In *Stones of Rimini*, Stokes applies Klein's concept of reparation to interpret Italian Renaissance architecture. His interpretations emphasize the visual features of design and the architectural expression of universal psychical positions, the manic and the depressive. Looking at Italian Renaissance architecture through the lens of Klein's psychical positions, Stokes defines two traditions in Italian Renaissance architecture: carving and modeling. Carving and modeling are interdependent, often occurring in the same building. The carving tradition emphasizes the cutting away of material to reveal the intrinsic nature of the material, attention to the nature of the material, and handcraft. In the carving tradition, the artist emphasizes the intrinsic qualities of a material, the "smooth and rough" qualities of the material, and ultimately strives for a unified "mass effect." The modeling tradition, on the other hand, emphasizes "design," form, or idea over the intrinsic nature of the material and emphasizes an additive building-up of form based on an aggregation of parts. In the modeling tradition, artists force the material to conform to "preconceived" notions. Stokes says this leads to a kind of willful abstraction resulting in a lack of internal coherence (Stokes, 1932: 108–110, 118–120). Stokes suggests that the contrasting traditions are universal to the arts and architecture, and he theorized that is so because of underlying conflicting emotions surrounding the loss and need for reparation in childhood to which Klein called attention. Modeling is less reparative because in that tradition a material substance such as stone is not accepted for what it actually is. And that is why, for Stokes, the modeling tradition stems from the difficulty in infancy to eventually accept the mother, and perhaps the self, as separate and "whole" beings. In *The Quattro*

Cento, 1932, Stokes elaborates. A key example is the Palazzo Ducale Courtyard, Urbino, 1467–1472, by Luciano Laurana. Smooth and rough qualities of the courtyard express "separation and synthesis" where the rough brick and mortar walls of the courtyard are punctuated by window openings "bitten" from the walls and highlighted by smooth stone moldings. The distinct parts, smooth and rough, and carved and modeled, make a unified whole (Stokes, 1932: 155–158). Thus, for Stokes, architecture can echo mother and child phantasies in infancy in which objects that represent the mother are "punished" and "roughed up" for behaving badly and express reparation that reconstitutes the mother and the self as "loved and yet separate objects." The smooth and rough parts of architecture, when integrated as a unified whole architectural object, represent the psychical history of the universal positions of infancy. Smooth and rough parts combined in a unified whole offer the possibility to unconsciously affirm reparation and in so doing also offer the possibility for a satisfying aesthetic experience.

One of the potential limitations in using Klein's idea of reparation for aesthetic interpretation is that Klein blurred what Freud regarded to be distinct episodes or phases of development in infancy. A related problem stems from Klein's emphasis on persecutory part-objects coinciding with the earliest or first psychical "position" in infancy. That emphasis can lead to the assumption that, even in early infancy, the infant takes objects to be objects, i.e., as if the infant thinks "that object is a nipple, its mine, and sometimes it's defiant." However, in Freud's account of the oral phase, the infant has an object (the breast/ mother) but the infant is not aware of it as such. Freud writes "(o)riginally the ego includes everything, later it separates off an external world from itself. Our present ego feeling is, therefore, only a shrunken residue of a much more inclusive – indeed all embracing – feeling which corresponds to a more intimate bond between the ego and the world about it" (Freud, 1930: 254). The discussion will return to Freud's thought on the earliest experience of selfhood in Chapter 4. Here, the aim is simply to note distinctions that have implications for architectural theory and practice, and how to reliably draw from Freud, as distinct from Freudian psychoanalysts who like Klein strove to build on Freud's work.

Inside-outside corners, birth trauma, and character armor

Richard Neutra (1892–1970) began developing modern house designs in Los Angeles, CA, in the late 1940s for clients amenable to psychoanalytic ideas. Sylvia Lavin, in *Form Follows Libido*, 2004, describes Neutra as an architect who saw himself as a psychotherapeutic designer. Uniquely, Neutra based his design ideas on therapy and birth trauma, as theorized by Freudian psychoanalysts Otto Rank (1884–1939), and character armor, as theorized by Wilhelm Reich (1897–1957). Rank was a colleague of Freud's, but Freud broke with Rank over the issue of birth trauma, viewing Rank's ideas on birth trauma as unsupportable (Freud, 1926). Neutra interpreted Rank's notion that birth and the house are linked as symbols "of the creative ego...freed...from the maternal protective covering" where selfhood is bonded on the one hand to interiority (being inside the womb) and on the other hand exteriority (being outside the womb). Neutra believed a house should mirror that sense of selfhood (Lavin, 2004: 54–55). For example, with the Rourke House by Neutra, 1949, inside-outside relationships are framed by a rectangular house form, a glass wall that opens the interior to the outside, and a flat roof extending out over the exterior beyond the glass wall, thereby reinforcing both interiority and exteriority (Lavin, 2004: 59–62).

Similarly, the influence of the psychoanalyst Wilhelm Reich on Neutra is expressed in the Moore House, 1952, and the Chuey House, 1956. Reich published *Character Analysis* in 1933 and *The Function of the Orgasm* in 1945. Reich was a highly controversial psychoanalyst who invented an Orgone Accumulator. The accumulator was a human-sized enclosure intended to focus orgone radiation on an inhabitant. Reich alone believed in orgone radiation and thought it to be an atmospheric energy source that could heighten libido and, when combined with sexual gratification, would prevent if not cure cancer, reduce anxiety and physical tension, and help overcome physical and psychical rigidities that combine to make a person's defensive character armor. Many analysts, including Freud, saw defensive behavioral traits as defensive screens and obstacles to therapeutic treatment. Neutra supposed houses could be designed to reduce anxiety, psychological barriers, and physical tension, much like orgone accumulators. The Moore House and the Chuey House, Lavin notes, express the cumulative influences of both Rank and Reich on Neutra's design thinking. Both houses frame inside-outside relationships with a rectangular house-form; transparent glass walls define corners that open to the outside, and those corners are accentuated by spider-leg framing extending a flat roof out over the exterior well beyond the glass to reinforce interiority as well as exteriority (Lavin, 2004: 96, 110).

Many analysts, including Freud, saw defensive behavioral traits as defensive screens and obstacles to therapeutic treatment. Neutra supposed houses could be designed to reduce anxiety …and physical tension…

Though Rank and Reich were mentored by Freud early in their careers, they developed unorthodox ideas that, though transferable to architecture, do not reflect the robustness of Freud's system of thought outlined in Chapter 1 and Chapter 2 on selfhood and trauma, psychical developments after birth, the theory of psychical representation, and therapeutic technique for treating neuroses. Freud focused on the treatment of neuroses and to a lesser extent on the interpretation of culture. As suggested above, Rank and Reich became more concerned with environmental factors that could be leveraged to prevent neuroses. Neutra, the architect, was logically more interested in the latter. Neutra was most interested in architecture's psychological agency, the psychological affordances his designs could provide to clients who were not actually his "patients" but who were familiar with and looked favorably on psychoanalytic ideas. This led Neutra to design houses that combined closed-form and open-form areas, a combination that was appreciated by his clients. However, it is not difficult to imagine that others might experience anxiousness in the closed-form areas of Neutra's houses (e.g., too restrictive, claustrophobic) or in the open-form areas (e.g., too exposed, agoraphobic). As shall be explained in Chapters 4 and 5, Freud's system of thought suggests that there are theoretically grounded reasons for such responses.

The turbulent section and the paranoid critical method

In "Dali and Le Corbusier, the Paranoid Critical Method," 1978, Rem Koolhaas, (b. 1944), architect and theorist, reflects on psychical structures that influence the creative design practices of Dali and Le Corbusier. Koolhaas' idea is that all people, including architects, share a type of psychical structure, a paranoid critical structure, that influences creative practices. Drawing from psychoanalytic theory on paranoia, Koolhaas theorizes that the architect, like the paranoiac, "turns the whole world into a magnetic field of facts, all pointing in the same direction." Architecture, Koolhaas writes, is "inevitably a form of PC [paranoid critical] activity." Similarly, he suggests, marketing and reception of designed objects, as well as material culture, arrange information in ways that, like iron filings in a magnetic field, trace psychical force fields (Koolhaas, 1978: 155, 161).

Thus, with one eye on psychoanalytic theory and the other on architecture, Koolhaas views the delirium of paranoia as part of a behavioral continuum ranging from normal to abnormal. From a psychoanalytic point of view, that idea is not as wild as it might seem. As explained in Chapter 1, Freud said "an unbroken chain bridges the gap between the neuroses in all their manifestations and normality" (Freud, 1905 (1920): 171). And so, in the material culture of Manhattan, Koolhaas observes, delirium is not so much a problem as it is an engine for culture, an engine that has been leveraged for creative innovation. The delirium is reflected in the New York Athletic Club tower, "a turbulent stacking of metropolitan life...a machine...a surfeit of hedonism, a conventional, even boring skyscraper, and a program as daring as ever could be imagined" (Koolhaas, 1991: 161). Koolhaas has drawn on these ideas as inspiration for creative and interpretive projects in his professional practice Koolhaas/OMA. For example, Très Grande Bibliothèque, 1989, competition proposal is marked by a turbulent stacking of activity areas that are open to each other. Koolhaas's ideas are examined more closely in Chapter 7.

...with one eye on psychoanalytic theory and the other on architecture, Koolhaas views the delirium of paranoia as part of a behavioral continuum ranging from normal to abnormal. From a psychoanalytic point of view, that idea is not as wild as it might seem.

Asymmetric blur zones and the uncanny

Blurred Zones, 2003, by Peter Eisenman, architect and theorist, leverages the language of psychoanalytic theory to suggest that the unconscious adds to the understanding of architecture as well as creative practice, particularly Eisenman's creative practice. _Blurred Zones_ represents a more recent example of the longstanding architectural interest in how the unconscious contributes to aesthetic intuition and particularly design creativity. Like Koolhaas, Neutra, and Moholy-Nagy, Eisenman suggests that an architect can intentionally create designs that account for the unconscious, its structures, and its mechanisms of psychical representation. For Eisenman, the Rebstockpark housing masterplan is a case in point. His design for that project includes an asymmetrical 3-dimensional matrix and faceted slab-like buildings. The surfaces of each slab vary subtly in ways that echo the faceted features of adjacent slabs. The slabs and void spaces between slabs throughout vie for figure-ground prominence like an ambigram, establishing what Eisenman calls "blurred zones." Eisenman says the blurred zones are characterized by "neither figure nor ground but aspects of both." Blurred-zones experiences, he writes, are linked to an "unconscious world of presences." Further, blurred zones appeal to a "more pure desire...opening up the realm of the unconscious where desire operates...a blurred condition between form and content" (Eisenman, 2003: 8–9, 132). The Rebstockpark design is examined more closely in Chapter 4.

Whereas Eisenman, like Koolhaas, leverages psychoanalytic concepts to generate nontraditional architectural ideas and designs, Anthony Vidler leverages psychoanalytic concepts to suggest that nontraditional designs like those by Koolhaas and Eisenman mentioned above are harmful. Vidler's *The Architectural Uncanny*, 1992, and *Warped Space*, 2000, are important points of reference for psychoanalytically informed interpretations of art and architecture, particularly modern architecture. As mentioned in Chapter 1, psychoanalytic theory has been applied to interpret artistic production that conflicts with anthropocentric ideals and to judge nonconforming design or style as deviant if not perverse. *The Architectural Uncanny* and *Warped Space* are compelling examples of that approach. Similar to Wölfflin, discussed earlier in this chapter, Vidler subscribes to the idea that buildings should mirror the human body even if only abstractly, perhaps through symmetry and proportion. The problem, Vidler suggests, is that the classic anthropomorphic model of architecture has been abandoned by modern architecture "with uncanny consequences" (Vidler, 1990 (1996): 575. Vidler, 1992: 77). The consequences, Vidler suggests, are that modern architecture and urban space cause people to feel disembodied and disturbed.

Vidler intends his criticism as a direct reference to "The Uncanny," written by Freud, 1919. However, the theoretical support for Vidler's criticism actually stems from early-modern social criticisms of modernity, the modern city, and modern architecture, rather than from Freud or psychoanalytic theory. As Vidler says, "most analysts have basically agreed with him [Freud] on the secondary, or displaced, role of the environment in agoraphobia...and yet for the purposes of architectural and urban interpretation, in a context of the cultural understanding of space, we might rather insist that these secondary roles are primary" (Vidler, 2000: 40). In further support of his approach, in "The Psychopathologies of Modern Space: Metropolitan Fear from Agoraphobia to Estrangement," Vidler offers a historical synopsis of the cultural context in which spatial neurosis came to be identified with modernity and the modern city. He suggests that because modernity and the modern city were regarded by social critics as metaphors of estrangement, modernity and the modern city actually produced psychoneuroses and phobias such as agoraphobia (Vidler, 1994: 11–29). However, as noted in this chapter and in Chapter 1, Freud maintained that "an unbroken chain

52   AESTHETIC EXPERIENCE

bridges the gap between the neuroses in all their manifestations and normality." What some might view as perversion "is itself of no rarity but must form a part of what passes as the normal" (Freud, 1905 (1920): 171).

Conclusion

Chapter 3 has outlined how architecture theorists and designers have sought to understand aesthetic intuition, explored the idea that people unconsciously experience and identify with architecture and why that might lead to pleasing or displeasing experiences. The discussion began with key examples before Freud, such as Gottfried Semper, and finished with Anthony Vidler's suggestion that modern architecture creates neuroses because it has abandoned anthropomorphic traditions and conventions. The discussion highlighted key issues and contrasting perspectives on aesthetic experience. In the more recent examples, Freud and psychoanalytic concepts have been recruited to support contrasting views regarding what is praiseworthy and what is not. The contrast between Koolhaas and Vidler is rather striking in that regard. Such differences raise questions about how Freud's ideas can be reliably applied to interpret architecture and conclusions that can be drawn. Certainly, Freud cautioned against defining normality and abnormality too narrowly.

Chapters 4–7 explore Freud's thought on how the phases of development in childhood influence selfhood. His thoughts suggest that adult self-image and aesthetic intuition are not reducible to the anthropomorphic body image. On the other hand, Freud's thought suggests that humans are well prepared psychically to appreciate both closed-form and open-form architecture. This insight has implications for the architectural understanding of form and formlessness, as well as preferences for and against architectural convention.

CHAPTER 4

Open form, the formless, and "that oceanic feeling"

Chapter 4 draws from Freud to explore the empathy for open form and formlessness in architecture. Moholy-Nagy's "space relationships" drawing and Peter Eisenman's Rebstockpark housing masterplan are the primary architectural examples. Eisenman's imaginative description of "blurred zones" lends itself to the exploration of issues that are expressed more simply in Moholy-Nagy's drawing created many years earlier. Freud's observations on the oral phase of development in childhood help explain why the architect, or anyone else, might have empathy for open form and formlessness and "oceanic" feelings of oneness with everything around them.

Freud's observations on the oral phase of development in childhood help explain why the architect, or anyone else, might have empathy for open form and formlessness and "oceanic" feelings of oneness with everything around them.

Architectural formlessness, not literal formlessness

Common sense suggests that architecture cannot actually be formless, that architecture can at most only express the human empathy for formlessness, or perhaps empathy for an oceanic sense of oneness with the world. That is, if architecture can express empathy for formlessness, it can do so only with the means available to it as architecture. That notion is rather succinctly illustrated by

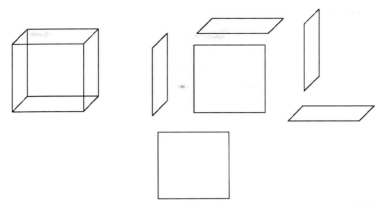

Figure 2 Closed form versus "space relationships," László Moholy-Nagy, 1928, redrawn: intuition of open form and formlessness.

Moholy-Nagy's "space relationships" drawing (Figure 2). Moholy-Nagy's original space relations drawing has been redrawn here to facilitate comparison with other drawings in this chapter and other chapters.

The cube on the left in Moholy-Nagy's drawing is a closed form, and visually the emphasis is on the idea of a cube. A cube, as such, lacks any intrinsic directionality (left, right, etc.). However, the axonometric drawing of this cube presents us with a "front" face and so invites us to look at it frontally. From this vantage point, one also sees a left side, right side, a back side. Without these left and right hand references to our own body, the cube would have no intrinsic directionality. Describing this object in terms of front-back or left-right is already an indication that a bodily identification with the cube has occurred. The "front" is the plane that "faces" us. In this way, the cube becomes an object that mirrors human form, even if only abstractly. Mentally, we blur distinctions between our body and the cube, and thus the cube acquires the directionality of our own body, though we understand that it is not our body. We can imagine what it would be like to be inside the cube, or stand beside it, but to do so we would need to imagine size relationships, for example, the size of the cube. More formally, as described here the cube reflects the traditional idea that architecture is nothing if not a bodily form, and like the human body architecture form is enclosed form.

Alternatively, looking at the right side of Moholy-Nagy's drawing and the scattered planes to the right of the cube, there does not appear to be a closed form so much as an asymmetrical array of planes. The scattered planes do not make a "form" so much as they represent the idea of space relationships, or perhaps the scattered planes represent an indeterminate form of space relationships. Unlike the cube, the scattered group of planes do not lend themselves to associations with human body form. The drawing presents something other than a simple separation of the sides of the cube. Due to the way Moholy-Nagy drew and arranged them, the planes appear to switch back and forth from foreground to background depending on what our eyes focus on. Thus, the space relationships drawn on the right suggest a kind of movement toward formlessness without actually being formless. With this drawing, Moholy-Nagy illustrates his empathy for the space relationships on the right in contrast with the closed form on the left.

The drawing is an outcome of Moholy-Nagy's creative introspective attempts to access his "subconscious." That led him to believe that his empathy for the space relations shown on the right in the drawing stems from psychical forces and that the lines somehow outline his empathy. In *The New Vision*, 1928, he explains:

"[t]he intuitive is most accurately understood as a speeded up, subconscious logic.... Here lies the ineffable. This kind of experience is fundamentally non-verbal but it is not inarticulate to the visual and other senses.... I learned that the manner in which lines are related, not objects as such, carry the richer message" (Moholy-Nagy, 1928: 68–71).

Clearly, for Moholy-Nagy, the drawing represents a highly nuanced set of relationships. The drawing represents the "subconscious" psychical intuition of "relations extending in all directions" (Moholy-Nagy, 1928: 59-64). The drawing expresses his wish to visualize that "experience" in the external world, to project the intuition outwardly through drawing. And the drawing expresses a wish to experience that "ineffable" spatiality in the external world by means of empathy for space relationships, "not objects as such." Though Moholy-Nagy can intuit ineffable space relations, a drawing can only represent his empathy for it. That is, the lines can only represent the ineffable, and as is the case with formlessness, the drawing, like architecture, cannot literally be formless. Freud's system of thought helps explain what Moholy-Nagy refers to as the subconscious logic of the architectural empathy for open form and the formless.

Freud and the spatialities of the psychical apparatus

Freud's thought on the psychical apparatus and selfhood in the first phase of development in infancy helps explain how architectural designs can arise as projections of the intuition and empathy for open form and formlessness, and how the unconscious might be implicated in the reception and creative design of architectural objects.

Freud describes the spatialities of the psychical apparatus in *The Ego and the Id*, 1923, in which he identifies major divisions of the psyche: the conscious, preconscious, unconscious, ego, id, and superego. These are what he diagrams as differentiations that make up the system of the "mental apparatus" (Freud 1923a: 24-25). The ego rests on the "surface" of the id but does not completely "envelope" it. The id is a "great reservoir" of pleasure seeking impulses (Freud, 1923a: 30). The id seeks pleasure and is opportunistic, and the ego does its bidding. The ego is "like a man on horseback...obliged to guide it [the id] where it wants to go; so in the same way the ego is in the habit of transforming the id's will into action as if it were its own" (Freud, 1923a: 25). The ego in each phase represents an "identification" with the unique impulses in each phase. In that way, the ego is what the child in the phase experiences as selfhood, a combination of self-experience and self-image in each phase associated with the unique impulses in each phase (Freud, 1923a: 28-29).

In *Beyond the Pleasure Principle*, 1920, Freud suggests that the psychical apparatus and psychical ideas are programmatic, they are pleasure seeking and strategically so, in ways that have spatial implications. For example, Freud describes the psychical apparatus as a "shield" having a capacity to screen external stimuli and to organize the "projection" of impulses. "[T]he feelings of pleasure and unpleasure (which are an index to what is happening in the interior of the apparatus) predominates over all external stimuli" (Freud, 1920: 27). In projection, displeasure is treated as though it were "acting, not from the inside, but from the outside, so that it may be possible to bring a shield against stimuli into operation as a means of defense. This is the origin of projection" (Freud, 1920: 29). In other words, "projection" functions as a kind of parachute filled by the wind of internal impulses that both 'defends' against unpleasurable internal impulses and leads one on. Troubling impulses are displaced by projection onto 'outside' objects that then might be 'avoided.' Pleasing impulses are also projected onto outside objects, whereby objects become 'attractive'.

In *Beyond the Pleasure Principle*, 1920, Freud suggests that the psychical apparatus and psychical ideas are programmatic, i.e., they are pleasure seeking and strategically so, in ways that have spatial implications.

Phases of psychical development in childhood

In *Three Essays*, 1905 (1920), "The Unconscious," 1915, and "Mourning and Melancholia," 1917, Freud explains that unconscious psychical ideas in adulthood are linked in various ways to the phases of psychical development in infancy. Each phase marks a unique ego or self-image that represents a primary form of "identification" that defines selfhood in each phase. Selfhood in each phase arises from a particular set of relationships including an instinctual motivation or "impulse," a dominant body part, an external object, and a particular kind of work for dealing with the impulse. There are 5 main phases, the oral, anal, phallic, latency, and genital phase, from infancy to puberty. The latency phase precedes puberty and essentially inherits behavioral characteristics from earlier phases, and for that reason, the focus here shall be on the oral, anal, phallic, and genital phases. In each of those phases, a "psychical representative" idea or "ideational representative" of instinctual impulses expresses the "demand made on the mind for work" by impulses in the phase. In each phase, a particular part of the body, e.g., the mouth in the oral phase, is primarily associated with impulses in the phase and the experience of selfhood in the phase (Freud, 1905 (1920): 168, 197–198. Freud, 1915c: 177–178. Freud, 1917a: 249).

Freud explains that unconscious psychical ideas in adulthood are linked in various ways to the phases of psychical development in infancy. Each phase marks a unique ego or self-image that represents a primary form of "identification" that defines selfhood in each phase.

In *The Ego and the Id*, 1923, Freud explains that, in the final phase of infancy, a part of the ego becomes a "superego." While the early identifications in each phase contribute to the differentiation of the ego, or rather to the different identifications that characterize the ego as it passes through the phases, the rise of the superego in the genital phase represents one last identification. The last identification is with the parents, particularly the watchful eye of the parents which the child identifies with prohibitions against impulses in all earlier phases. The superego overrules the earlier ego identifications and impulses in each phase. Consequently, the superego is a substitute for the parents and becomes the locus of reaction formations that serve as defensive systems of thought such as morality, ideals, authoritative models, critical judgment, and persecutory agencies of watching and measuring, as well as obsessional and compulsive ideas and practices. This explains how all earlier identifications remain in the adult psyche but are subordinate to the superego, which rules over them. The superego is responsible for reaction formations against earlier impulses and defenses against the return of abandoned impulses. Thus, any particular adult can express impulses, or empathy for impulses, in any or all earlier phases, and the superego defends against indulgences with defensive systems of thought and avoidance behaviors (Freud, 1923a: 28–35, 45–46, 53–54). The superego explains why an architect, or anyone else, might express empathy for an architectural object that points through a chain of associations to the last phase of development, as well as back to earlier phases. The identifications with objects in the different phases remain in the adult psyche but are subordinate to the superego, which rules over them. Freud noted that repression and identification in each phase, as well as adulthood dispositions that often define adult character types, are normal (Freud, 1913: 323). That notion fits logically with Freud's general aim to define the "innate constitutional roots of the sexual instinct" that are "innate in *everyone*" (Freud's italics), whereby he maintained that "an unbroken chain bridges the gap between the neuroses in all their manifestations and normality" (Freud, 1905 (1920): 171).

The oral phase

Freud's account of selfhood the earliest phase, the oral phase, offers much to the understanding of the architectural empathy for open form and formlessness. In the oral phase, the infant acquires its first self-image (Freud, 1905 (1920): 198). The infant's "object" is the mother's breast, routinely involving suckling, whereby the primary sensory organ is the mouth and the primary experience is oral experience. Though the breast can be described objectively as an "object," the infant does not experience the breast as an "object." Instead, for the infant, the experience is such that there are no distinctions between the self and the breast or the mother or the external world. At that time, early in the oral phase, the infant does "not distinguish his ego from the external world." Rather "[o]riginally the ego includes everything, later it separates off an external world from itself" (Freud, 1930: 66, 68). That sense of selfhood is "the prototype of every relation of love. The finding of an object is a refinding of it" (Freud, 1905

(1920): 222). And "oceanic" feelings of oneness with the world in adulthood express the intimate ego–world bond that defines the first self-image in infancy. Later, in subsequent phases of development, selfhood becomes increasingly differentiated from the external world (Freud, 1930: 66, 68, 72).

…early in the oral phase, the infant does "not distinguish his ego from the external world." Rather "[o]riginally the ego includes everything, later it separates off an external world from itself."

Repression

In "Repression," 1915, and "The Unconscious," 1915, and in *The Ego and the Id*, 1923, Freud explains that repression is a special mechanism for the transition from one phase of development to another. He writes, "*the essence of repression lies simply in turning something away, and keeping it at a distance, from the conscious*" (Freud's italics, 1915b: 147). Repression involves abandoning the primary "object" and the sense of self associated with that object to move on to the next phase. Through repression, the impulses and the object toward which impulses trend are repressed and thus buried and abandoned in the unconscious. Through repression, ego identification in each phase partly defines the unconscious. The repressed remains in the unconscious as a shadow or ghost of the former ego and sense of selfhood. The process of repression is "a matter of a withdrawal," of abandoning and repressing primary objects and the psychical ideas linked to the objects (Freud, 1915c: 180). As such "[t]he repressed is the prototype of the unconscious" and a primary object defines the unconscious as if a ghost of the abandoned object (Freud, 1923a: 15). Thus, Freud says, the "shadow of the object falls on the ego" (Freud, 1917a: 249).

In "Repression," 1915, "The Transformation of Instinct…," 1917, and "Character and Anal Eroticism," 1908, Freud explains that repression enables a psychically ideational chain of associations in which primary objects and ideas are interchangeable in the unconscious. Adult object relations can point back through the ideational chain of associations to any one of the phases of psychosexual development and the character traits attributable to each. In the extreme case of neuroses, disabling symptoms signal the "*return of the repressed*" (Freud's italics, 1915b: 154–155). Further, Freud explains, the psychical origin of the idea of beauty as well as artistic activities are implicated in ideational chains of association that hark back to one or another phase in the development of selfhood (Freud, 1917b: 131–132. Freud, 1908a: 173–174). And, in so far as "space may be the projection…of the psychical apparatus" (Freud, 1941: 300), Freud's thought suggests that architectural expressions of empathy for open form and formlessness are involved in a chain of unconscious ideational associations to selfhood in the oral phase of infancy where "[o]riginally the ego includes everything."

Blurred zones and architectural empathy for formlessness

Freud's thought on the first phase of development in infancy suggests where the empathy for blurred zones might stem from and why anyone might experience that kind of architecture as pleasurable.

The Rebstockpark masterplan (Figure 3), a public sector housing proposal, is characterized by an asymmetrical pattern made up of intricately faceted slab forms. While each slab form represents a building, altogether the buildings make a kind of geological pattern. The volumes between slabs appear to ghost the slab forms, as if parts of an original solid geological formation have been removed, leaving voids that define the remaining slabs. Like rock formations, the surfaces of the remaining slabs trace the crystalline matrix from which they emerged and express the subtle dynamics of the virtually endless matrix. Thus, each freestanding slab is different from the others and yet expresses continuity with the others. In that way, each slab and the volumes between slabs express a kind of formlessness attributable to the organizing matrix. The matrix is not visible, rather it is suggested by the pattern of solids and voids. Solids and voids

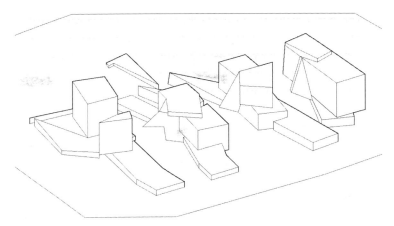

Figure 3 Blurred zone buildings, Rebstockpark masterplan, Peter Eisenman, 2003, redrawn: architectural empathy for formlessness, not literal formlessness.

vie for prominence like an ambigram to establish what Eisenman refers to as architectural "blurred zones" (Eisenman, 2003: 8–9).

Like Moholy-Nagy's "space relationships" drawing, the Rebstockpark design points toward formlessness. And, in the sense that Moholy-Nagy's drawing is motivated by an "inner urge," Eisenman's idea is that "blurred zones" express an "unconscious world of presences." Further, a "more pure desire…opening up the realm of the unconscious where desire operates" is integral to the blurred zones. Crucially, for Eisenman, his design for the Rebstockpark masterplan defines "a blurred condition between form and content." That, he says, involved clearing away obstacles to the unconscious by abandoning the traditional "metaphysics of presence" in architecture (Eisenman, 2003: 8–9). For Eisenman, the intuition of blurred zones involves abandoning the notions that architecture is defined by construction materials and that architecture should only represent human body form.

Looking at Eisenman's description of blurred zones through the lens of Freud's thought is illuminating. For example, Eisenman's motivation to create blurred zones suggests an intuitive understanding of an ideational chain of associations harking back to the oral phase of selfhood where firstly "the ego includes everything" and a formless-form of selfhood is "the prototype of every relation of love." Eisenman's desire for and discovery of blurred zones suggests empathy for the prototype of the intimate ego–world bond in the oral phase, if not a "refinding" of that relationship with primary objects in the oral phase (Freud, 1930: 66, 68. Freud, 1905 (1920): 222). Of course, like the oxymoronic circumstances of early childhood in which the ego is not yet differentiated from objects in the external world, blurred zones architecture could only be an ideational representation of the unconscious intuition of the formless-form prototype of selfhood in the oral phase. The psychical apparatus provides the unconscious chain of ideational associations that connect blurred zones to that prototype. In that way, the architecture expresses the empathy for formlessness in various ways, without literally being formless.

Preferences and preoccupations with formless-form are not the only potential effects of unconscious ideational associations harking back to the oral phase. Design strategies may also be implicated, the thoughts and techniques involved in creating a design. Ideational materials, e.g., theoretical references, may also be "ideational representative[s]" that express the "demand made on the mind for work" by impulses in any particular phase of development in childhood (Freud, 1905 (1920): 166, 197. 1915c: 177). The ego of the designer is "obliged to guide it [the id] where it wants to go; so in the same way, the ego is in the habit of transforming the id's will into action as if it were its own" (Freud, 1923a: 17–25).

Preferences and preoccupations with formless-form are not the only potential effects of unconscious ideational associations harking back to the oral phase. Design strategies may also be implicated, the thoughts and techniques involved in creating a design.

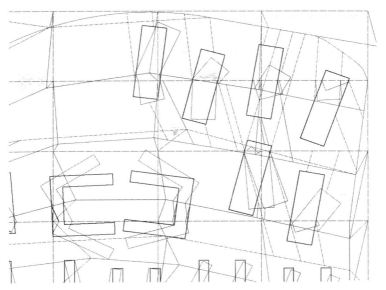

Figure 4 Plan, blurred zone matrix, Rebstockpark, Peter Eisenman, 2003, redrawn: a "realm of the unconscious where desire operates."

Through the lens of Freud's thought, the abstract 3-dimensional matrix that Eisenman invented to transform conventional housing forms into a masterplan of blurred zones can be interpreted as an ideation representative of unconscious "demands made on the [architect's] mind for work" by oral phase impulses. That demand is reflected in Eisenman's project narrative which reveals that he created and used the matrix as a tool for "opening up the realm of the unconscious where desire operates" enabling him to realize "a blurred condition between form and content."

Technically, the Rebstockpark matrix shown in Figure 4 is made up of 2 primary grids, one a flat orthogonal grid, and another grid below it that is a warped version of the top grid. Connecting those grids are torqued and trussed grids that are oriented perpendicular to the top and bottom grids. These torqued grids are created by connecting lines to corresponding points on the top and bottom grids. For Eisenman, the matrix represents blurred zones where architecture can be created and where matter like the slab-forms can change state. The solid–void pattern that emerges is "neither figure nor ground but aspects of both...a non-dialectical third condition, one which...reconstitutes the nature of both" (Eisenman, 2003: 132).

Eisenman sees the solids and voids making up the blurred zones of the Rebstockpark masterplan as a phase condition, as when water vapor changes into dew or ice or when a wave top becomes a white cap. Ideationally, for Eisenman, solids and voids in the matrix represent "temporal modulations" that express potentials for "the continual variation of matter" (Eisenman, 2003: 131). The connotation is that slab-form figures in the matrix are both obscure and distinct; they arise from a field of relations in the matrix and so are distinct from the matrix, but insofar as the slab-forms are fully determined by the matrix, they cannot be differentiated from it. Eisenman draws from the theories of Rene Thom and Gilles Delueze to elaborate the notion that the Rebstockpark slab-forms express how water vapor can revert back to the oceanic matrix from which it emerged. Similarly, Eisenman highlights the idea that there are no essential forms, only infinite variations or "extensions" of material matter folding forward to give rise to form and backward to undo form. Eisenman imagines that a blurred zone matrix represents the potential to form material matter, and the potential to undo form, if not undo "repression" associated with form (Eisenman, 2003: 131–132). In that way, Eisenman leverages theoretical ideas drawn from Thom and Delueze to support his intuition of blurred zones as a "realm of the unconscious where desire operates." Looking at Eisenman's ideas through the lens of Freud's thought helps explain how even highly nuanced and theoretically motivated design strategies may be ideational representatives of unconscious "demands made on the [architect's] mind for work" by oral phase impulses. An unconscious chain of ideational associations may connect architectural form to an undifferentiated oceanic matrix from which selfhood emerged in the oral phase of development. Similarly, architectural form-making may be motivated by impulses in that phase.

Ideationally, for Eisenman, solids and voids in the matrix represent "temporal modulations" that express potentials for "the continual variation of matter"…the potential to form material matter, and the potential to undo form, if not undo "repression" associated with form…a "realm of the unconscious where desire operates."

Conclusion

Doubts about the capacity of the architectural object to be formless, or that buildings express the impulses of early infancy, are understandable. It would seem a contradiction to say that a thing is both an object and formless, or that dwelling can be unhinged from enclosing. Moreover, it might seem comical to suggest that an adult can enjoy a building in the way that an infant in the oral phase enjoys the nipple. After all, it is difficult to imagine what it was like to be an infant in the oral phase; it is difficult to imagine formlessness. And the formless is hard to represent. It lacks boundaries that would enable one to see it and recognize it. Hence, architecture as such cannot be formless, though it may express the empathy for it. In that sense, open form and blurred zones veer away from closed form, pointing instead to "oceanic" selfhood in the oral phase of infancy.

CHAPTER 5

Closed-form, rule-based composition and control of the architectural gift

Chapter 5 draws from Freud to explore the architectural empathy for closed-form, rule-based composition and the notion that the architectural object is a gift that the architect controls. House II, 1969–1970, by Peter Eisenman, is the primary architectural example because it expresses empathy for closed-form, rule-based composition and the control of the architectural gift. A sampling of the original 36 diagrams for the project has been redrawn in Figure 5. The diagrams illustrate procedures whereby an abstract cubic form intended to represent a house is experimentally segmented again and again to produce increasingly segmented forms. Freud's observations on the second phase of development in childhood, the anal phase, help explain why architects, and others, might have empathy for closed-form architectural objects.

Freud's observations on the second phase of development in childhood…help explain why architects, and others, might have empathy for closed-form architectural objects.

The second phase of development, the anal phase, and struggles over control of a gift

In *Three Essays*, 1905 (1920), Freud describes the impulses of the anal phase of development, impulses that also influence adult character traits. The child in the anal phase closely identifies a special object, and struggles over the control

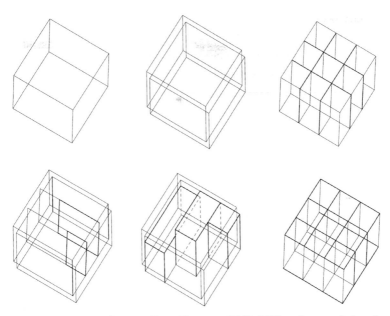

Figure 5 House II diagrams, Peter Eisenman, 1969–1970, redrawn: rule-based composition.

of the object and for dealing with it are at issue. The child takes self-centered pleasure in withholding and letting go of the object. The child exercises control over the object to increase pleasures associated with the object. And the child actively expresses compliance or noncompliance with the parents' demands regarding the object and control of the object. Naturally, for the infant in the anal phase, the object is the "contents of the bowels." Freud writes, the infant treats the object "as part of the infant's own body and represents his first 'gift.'" The gift is produced or not produced to express "compliance" with external demands or "disobedience" (Freud, 1905 (1920): 186). These circumstances define the ego or self-image as the child passes through the phase. Repression of relations with the object, stemming from the need to separate from and abandon identifications with the object give rise to "disgust" toward the once 'loved' object (Freud, 1905 (1920): 151, 222. Freud, 1908a: 171), as well as sadistic and masochistic ideations or phantasies associated with the object (Freud, 1905 (1920): 159, 226). These ideations are similar to those described in Chapter 2 in the outline of Melanie Klein's thoughts on the child's separation phantasies from the mother. The phantasies are such that the object is punished for being a bad object and where the punished object can retaliate. In adults, Freud observed that compulsive and obsessive preoccupations with cleanliness, decontamination rituals, as well as abusive treatment of special objects are unconsciously associated with anal impulses in infancy. Submission to abuses from special objects that are similarly associated with repressed impulses hark back through a chain of ideational association to anal phase identifications (Freud, 1905 (1920): 158–159). Moreover, adult "anal character" traits such as orderliness, parsimony, control behaviors and phantasies, obstinacy, and defiance hark back to selfhood in the anal phase. Though repression involves "abandoning" the special object in that phase and the repression of impulses and pleasures associated with the object, ideational condensations, displacements, and substitutions, such as compulsive and obsessive preoccupations with cleanliness, decontamination, and abusive treatment of special objects, signpost the influence of the anal phase on the adult (Freud, 1908a: 169–171).

<u>The child in the anal phase closely identifies with a special object, and struggles over the control of the object and for dealing with it are at issue. The child takes self-centered pleasure in withholding and letting go the object…treats the object "as part of the infant's own body and represent his first 'gift.'" The gift is produced or not produced to express "compliance" with external demands, or "disobedience."</u>

Threshold practices: isolation, repetition, procedures for handling objects, and diverting impulses

Threshold practices and strategies in adulthood, particularly in the compulsive and obsessive preoccupations that define neurosis or personality disorders, point to difficulties passing from the anal phase to the next phase of development. Freud mentions the notion of "threshold" and the symbolic meaning of threshold only in reference to dream content that anticipates transitioning from sleeping to waking, not in reference to compulsive and obsessive behaviors (Freud, 1900: 504). However, the word threshold is intended here to sum up Freud's observations on a host of compulsive and obsessive behaviors that establish psychical and physical boundaries. For example, he notes that "isolation" strategies involving preoccupation with establishing psychical and physical divisions or gaps in time or between objects are ideational representatives that hark back through a chain of associations to the repression of anal-phase impulses. Repetition strategies also serve to separate by substitution. For example, Freud says, a repetition strategy represents an unconscious wish to reenact or reimagine troubling object relations with a different, untroubling outcome. In this case, the individual behaves as if the original troubling experience had not happened or could be changed by imagining it differently, substituting the reimagined relationship with the object for the troubling relationship. Thus, isolation and repetition represent unconscious wishes to divert attention from pleasures identified with repressed objects (Freud, 1926: 119–122, 163–164). In less extreme and normal developments, "so important for the growth of a civilized and normal individual" (Freud, 1905 (1920): 178), the impulses of any particular phase can take the form of "reaction formations" that combine and can "be regarded as the source of a number of our virtues," including "artistic disposition" (Freud, 1905 (1920): 238–239).

...the word threshold is intended here to sum up Freud's observations on a host of compulsive and obsessive behaviors that

establish psychical and physical boundaries. For example, he notes that "isolation" strategies involving preoccupation with establishing psychical and physical divisions or gaps in time or between objects are ideational representatives that hark back through a chain of associations to the repression of anal-phase impulses.

People with obsessive-compulsive disorders have difficulty with free association and spontaneous communication of whatever comes to mind including random, unfiltered, and seemingly unconnected thoughts and memories. That is because they unconsciously and vigilantly strive to isolate their temptations and to avoid contact with the things that cause the temptations to arise. Processing thoughts in terms of categories serve that goal. Random thoughts and free associations disrupt the categorical thinking strategies intended to isolate and protect against repressed temptations. The adoption of rules, regulations, and procedures for handling and relating to objects is a way of maintaining distance from potential impulses, memories, and temptations associated with "troubling" and repressed impulses. Nonetheless, like the screen memory explained in Chapter 2, threshold strategies owe their existence and significance to the repressed impulses and experiences with the primary object. Though impulses are countered by the strategies, it is precisely those strategies that can point to anal-phase impulses and struggle there over the control of a special "gift" object in that phase (Freud, 1908a: 169–171. Freud, 1926: 119–122, 163–164).

A brief history of closed-form, rule-based composition and control of the architectural gift

Eisenman's House II design procedures and descriptions of the project lend themselves to a further exploration of architectural empathy for closed-form, rule-based composition and the control of the architectural gift. However, House

II is not an isolated case. Rather, it is representative of a long history of similar preoccupations in architecture.

Historically, the architectural conception of closed form remains most closely identified with the idea of a finite material object. The human body is a closed form, as is a cube. Thus, for Wölfflin, a closed architectural form is one that has a "finite whole" with a self-contained "scaffolding" of part-to-whole relationships where part by part the whole is "graduated by rule." Proper closed-form architecture is "rigid" and systematic, not fluid or open-ended (Wölfflin, 1915: 124–154). In that way, Wölfflin expressed his belief that the experience of form is always determined by the experience of the human body. This led him to take the closed form of the body and the expression of "limit, order, and law" as ideals for architecture (Wölfflin, 1915: 135, 149).

Logically, the empathy for closed form contrasts with empathy for the formless (Chapter 4). Closed form emphasizes a form that is separate from its surroundings, where rules and controls define a framework that is divided, segmented, and otherwise partitioned part by part. Similarly, the composition of closed form is often associated with design procedures and rituals that are intended to establish order and orderly relationships and to regulate practice as an orderly activity.

Logically, the empathy for closed form contrasts with empathy for the formless.... Closed form emphasizes a form that is separate from its surroundings, where rules and controls define a framework that is divided, segmented, and otherwise partitioned part by part.

Historically, composition and order are 2 closely related aesthetic terms. It is hardly possible to comment on architectural design creativity without describing composition and order in the making of a design. As the *Oxford English Dictionary* suggests, order generally implies sorting, classification, or systemization of works and their elements. Composition emphasizes the production of a work, its assemblage by design, bringing together, and arrangement of the parts to constitute a whole.

Design composition can involve an additive process, as in the concern for the proper combinations of parts as suggested in *De Architectura* by Vitruvius, circa 30 BC. Design composition can also involve a subtractive process, as suggested by Eisenman's House II diagrams. In the additive process, given elements are assembled, usually according to rules, to form a mass. Subtractive composition may involve cutting, scooping, carving out, or systematically chipping away at a given object, a volume, or solid block, usually following rules. Similarly, subtractive compositional strategies such as squeezing, stretching, pressing, partitioning, and patterning may be employed. In both cases, rules exercise control over the object as well as the architect. Certainly, a wide range of combinations between these general extremes exist. Whether additive or subtractive, since Vitruvius presented *De Architectura* as a gift to Rome and architecture, design composition has been regarded as a gift the architect bestows on clients.

…since Vitruvius presented *De Architectura* as a gift to Rome and architecture, design composition has been regarded as a gift the architect bestows on clients.

Architects since Vitruvius have presented self-promoting treatises with graphic examples to visually appeal to the public for recognition of their architectural gifts, and accompanying descriptions explain why they should be recognized as such. The cunning self-promotional strategies documented in *Le Corbusier Oeuvre Complete* offer many examples (Boesiger, 1995). Beatriz Colomina suggests that self-promotional materials are how the modern architect constructs a self-image, seeing oneself in the promotional materials as if in a mirror, while also identifying with a broader public audience and appealing to that audience (Colomina, 1988). Certainly architects today exhibit their gifts and solicit recognition for them in exhibitions, journals, monographs, and internet web pages.

Everyday experience reveals that the architect and the architecture student sometimes express ambivalence toward their audience, e.g., client, design instructor, and public. This is commonly seen in struggles over the control of the design process and the design outcome, and over the evaluations, criticism, and judgments about designs. The options are to reject the demands of the audience, to negotiate a compromise, or simply to comply with the demands. Compliance and noncompliance behaviors are also implicated in struggles over control of the gift of composition. For the architect, the struggle is a matter of giving the gift to the client while somehow retaining it. That is, unconsciously, the question of how to give a gift-object and be recognized or loved for one's gifts. House II offers itself as an example of this ingenious logic of architecture in which the gift is given over to a client but is also retained somehow or identified as the architect's gift object. In such cases, a design projects the identity of the architect, not the client. In some cases, the client willingly supports this gift-logic, in which case the client acquires a "Frank Lloyd Wright house" or a "Norman Foster building," or, in the case of House II, the client acquires an Eisenman house.

…unconsciously, the question is how to give a gift-object and be recognized or loved for one's gifts.

House II

"House II," as a project name, is revealing in the sense that, like other houses in a series of house projects designed by Eisenman (Houses 1–11a, 1968–1980), the name of the client has been substituted for the generic name "House II." As the name suggests, the conventional expectations of a residential client have been excluded from design consideration. Instead, this house project serves as a demonstration of the architect's ideas and design techniques, and through publication of the house diagrams, the architect solicits public recognition for his gifts. Such strategies offer themselves as examples of what Freud called "ideational representatives" that express the "demand made on the mind for work" by impulses in any given phase (as introduced in Chapter 4 on the phases of development).

The volume in the upper left of the series of diagrams in Figure 5 is also telling. It shows the house is conceived, at least initially, as an abstract volume, a closed form with which to explore the internal logic or structure of architecture, not as a home. As such, the volume suggests empathy for a distilled version of architecture, reflecting preoccupations with what Freud calls "decontamination" as a type of "ideational representative" that harks back through a chain of associations to the anal phase of development in childhood.

That volume establishes the basis of many diagrammatic procedures, and only relatively simple examples are shown in Figure 5. In each case, a volume has been subjected to rule-based modifications. The modifications lead step by step to a final design. Looking at the diagrams, it is not difficult to imagine the rule-based procedures, otherwise known in computational architecture as algorithms: "Step 1, there shall be an abstract volume representing the pure form of a house, the height, width, and depth of the outlined volume shall be the only attributes of the volume, solids and void portions will be defined later, pay no attention to conventional expectations regarding home design. Step 2, repeat and offset the volume, place the offset volume slightly downward and to the right, place the result to the right of the first volume. Step 3, repeat the first volume, divide it into 9 parts, and place the result to the right of the second volume. Step 4, start a new row, and in the left position, below the first volume, repeat the volume in the middle of the upper row, divide the volume in 1 direction into 3 parts that align with the 9-part volume on the upper right. Step 5, in the second row, middle position, repeat the volume in the middle of the upper row and divide the volume in the other direction into 3 volumes that align with the 9-part volume on the upper right, and stagger the length of the volumes to align with the 9-part volume on the upper right," and so on. In this highly self-referential process, external issues are excluded; there is no depiction of the site for the house, no brief for human activity areas to be accommodated, e.g., entry, living room, or kitchen. Visually, the diagrams express empathy for repetitive division, partitioning, removal, and offsetting techniques that increasingly subdivide and ritualistically define what may be solid and what may be void. Such rule-based procedures suggest, as explained earlier, what Freud describes as ideational isolation and repetition strategies that hark back to anal-phase reaction formations, which can be "the source of a number of our virtues," including "artistic disposition."

…the diagrams express empathy for repetitive division, partitioning, removal, and offsetting techniques that increasingly subdivide and ritualistically define what may be solid and what may be void. Such rule-based procedures suggest…what Freud describes as ideational isolation and repetition strategies that hark back to anal phase…"the source of a number of our virtues," including "artistic disposition."

Aside from the graphically self-evident preoccupations with the internal segmentation of House II, for Eisenman, it is important that the house is built to assert its "criticality" in the external world. He writes, "[c]riticality evolves out of the possibility of both repetition, to know what has gone before, and difference, to be able to change that history." The point of repetition, he says, is not simply to be "unique"; rather the aim is to be "different from a manifestation in the past" (Eisenman, 1999: 37). Eisenman's description of criticality offers itself as an architecturally specific example of empathy for what

Freud calls repetition as an ideational representative of an unconscious wish to reenact or re-imagine troubling object relations with a different, untroubling outcome. In such cases, Freud says, repetition is motivated by the unconscious wish to reimagine the original troubling experience as if it had not happened, or as if it could be changed by imagining it differently, and perhaps "isolating" impulses identified with the anal phase.

Conclusion

This chapter has drawn from Freud to explore the empathy for closed-form architecture. Exploration included rule-based composition and control strategies, as well as self-promotional documentation to exhibit architectural "gifts" while soliciting recognition for gifts. House II diagrams by Eisenman were the primary architectural examples.

For the child in the anal phase, the struggle over the control of a special gift-object is at stake. Eventually, the child must abandon its attachment to the object. Repression of impulses associated with the object leads to abandoning the object. Reaction formations reinforce repression and are expressed in various ways including orderliness, parsimony, obstinacy, defiance, phantasy involving objects, as well as ideational decontamination and control strategies for handling objects, including isolation and repetition procedures.

The House II diagrams suggest architectural empathy for closed form and ideational decontamination and control strategies, including isolation and repetition procedures for handling objects. That is partly because the diagrams are intended to represent a distilled version of a house, and each diagram is based on a series of rule-based procedures that lead repetitively to increasingly segmented forms. The diagrams also establish the basis of self-promotional materials that serve to exhibit the architect's "critical" gifts while soliciting recognition for such gifts. Thus, the House II project diagrams tally with what Freud describes as ideational strategies that hark back through a chain of associations to the anal phase in infancy and selfhood in that phase.

CHAPTER 6

Architectural simulation: wishful phantasy and the real

Simulation has long enabled the architect to transfer wishful ideas in the mind's eye to graphic representations of ideas that can be shared with others in the external world. Simulation establishes a virtual space that is a phase apart from the real world, and so also affords a safe space to challenge and overcome obstacles in the real world, if not to critically challenge conventions, prohibitions, and taboos. The drawings discussed in Chapters 4 and 5 suggest how, through simulation, architecture can be imagined fancifully to critically challenge conventions. Like those drawings, "Vertical Horizon" by architect Daniel Libeskind, 1979, a part of which is shown below in Figure 6, is an example of critical simulation. However, Libeskind's drawing indulges more fancifully in the freedoms afforded by simulation. That is why "Vertical Horizon" is the primary architectural example in this chapter.

"Vertical Horizon" is fanciful partly because it does not represent architecture intended for construction in the real world beyond the drawing. That is not surprising because the drawing does not seem to outline a proper architectural object e.g., a building. There are many architectural bits or architectural elements, but they do not add up compositionally to make a whole building. Also, orthographic conventions for architectural drawings appear to have been randomly applied: some elements appear to have been drawn in plan, some in section, some bits are depicted from one vantage point, and other bits are viewed from other vantage points. These characteristics of "Vertical Horizon" suggest a kind of preoccupation with architectural simulation, rather than with a building design intended for construction. It is as if the object of architectural affection is drawing per se, perhaps because drawing supports simulation and the freedoms that the spatiality of simulation affords. Yet the

79   ARCHITECTURAL SIMULATION

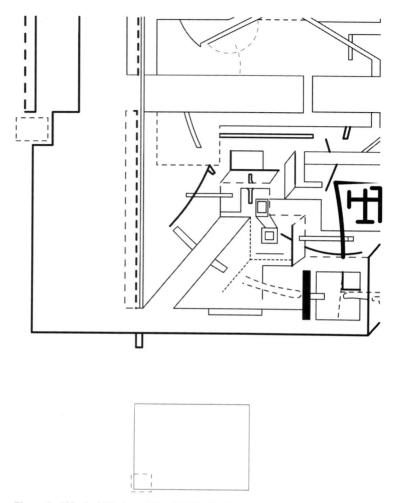

Figure 6 "Vertical Horizon," Daniel Libeskind, 1979, detail, area of detail indicated by square immediately above with dashed line around lower left corner, redrawn: wishful architectural simulation.

repetitive and emphatic representation of architectural elements in "Vertical Horizon" suggests that the architect believes "Vertical Horizon" is architecture or ought to be regarded as architecture. Thus, "Vertical Horizon" offers itself as an example of critical simulation because it simulates architecture in ways that critically challenge conventional notions about architecture. And further, it challenges conventional notions about what is proper for architectural simulation.

Freud's observations on the third phase of development in childhood help explain the architectural empathy for critical simulation as a means to explore wishful ideas, particularly critical simulation that combines reality and phantasy to overcome conventions, prohibitions, and taboos.

Freud's observations on the third phase of development in childhood help explain the architectural empathy for critical simulation as a means to explore wishful ideas, particularly critical simulation that combines reality and phantasy to overcome conventions, prohibitions, and taboos. Freud notes that, in the third phase of development in childhood, the phallic phase, the phallic phantasy has a defining influence on selfhood. In the phallic phantasy, the child casts itself in a phallic role, a role in which the child has its object of affection in the way that the child wants it. Essentially, the phallic phantasy is a phantasy of control and self-determination. Similarly, critical architectural simulation affords the opportunity to cast oneself as an architect in a phallic role, a role in which one designs a "world" with a special object and experiences the object in the way one wants it. In that sense, like the phallic phantasy, critical simulation in architecture is also a phantasy of control and self-determination.

The third phase of development, the phallic phase, a wish and overcoming prohibitions against the wish

In *Three Essays*, 1905 (1920), Freud describes the impulses of the phallic phase of development, impulses that influence adult character traits, as is the case with earlier phases. For the child in the phallic phase, a "wishful phantasy" features prominently as the ideational representative of impulses in that phase. In the phantasy, the child takes narcissistic (self-centered) enjoyment in impulses toward a special object. The child associates the impulses and the object with prohibitions and taboos against acting on impulses toward the object (Freud, 1905 (1920): 199–200, 225–227).

For the child in the phallic phase, a "wishful phantasy" features prominently as the ideational representative of impulses in that phase. In the phantasy, the child…associates the impulses and the object with prohibitions and taboos….

"Phantasy" is a psychoanalytic term for a fantasy that involves wish fulfillment, particularly wish fulfillment in relation to obstacles against fulfillment in the external world. Phantasy is one of a general group of psychical productions that Freud identifies with wish fulfillment, such as day dreams, reveries, sleep dreams, screen memories, and other ideational representatives involving condensation, substitution, and displacement (Freud, 1895: 218-19, 248–252,. Freud, 1908b: 147-147. Freud, 1916–1917: 370-373. Freud, 1905 (1920): 225–227). As such, phantasy is part of Freud's theory of psychical representation outlined in Chapter 2 in the discussion on Freud's "Architecture of Hysteria" diagram. While phantasy and fantasy are closely related, phantasy more closely captures Freud's meaning, which emphasizes imagination and psychical innovation rather than whimsy (Stratchey, 1966: xxiv).

Among all of Freud's observations on the phases of infancy, his thoughts on the phallic phase are perhaps the most controversial and most stereotyped in popular culture. That is partly because, for the child in the phallic phase, phantasy involves genital self-stimulation, also called masturbation. Further, the plot of the phantasy involves playing an active or passive role with regard to a special object of affection in the phase, one or another parent (Freud, 1905 (1920): 225–227. 1924: 176). Setting aside the most controversial and complex aspects of Freud's thought on this phase brings into focus the fundamental structure of the phallic phantasy, helping explain the architectural empathy for simulation.

In the phallic phase, a parent is chosen as the special object of affection. The child imagines itself to be in competition with the other parent for the affections of the chosen parent. The child believes that the competing parent represents an obstacle and prohibition against acting on impulses toward the chosen parent. The phallic phantasy arises as a substitute for wish fulfillment in the real world, a substitute for acting on impulses toward the object, and having the object in the way the child wants it. The ideational contents of the phantasy are directed toward the special object, and the phantasy becomes a way of circumventing obstacles in the real world against wishful impulses toward the object (Freud, 1905 (1920): 199–200, 225–227. Freud, 1923a: 31-32. Freud, 1924: 176).

Crucially, the phallic phantasy hinges on an approximation of reality, yet imagining a different reality in which obstacles and prohibitions are overcome, if not simply sidestepped. Another critical difference from reality is that the phantasy approximates wish fulfillment in the relative safety of the phantasy. Most importantly, in the phallic phantasy, the child casts itself in a role in which the child has its object of affection in the way that the child wants it. Thus, Freud says, the "primacy of the phallus" is at issue, "not the primacy of the genitals" (Freud, 1923b: 142). Hence, contrary to what is often assumed in popular culture, the phallus is not a genital so much as an ideational representative of control and self-determination, representing the ability to have the object of affection in the way one wants it. Similarly, in the unconscious symbolic language of the psyche, a phallic object is associated with prohibitions and taboos against phallic impulses. The plot of the phallic phantasy is to have and experience the object of affection virtually.

83   ARCHITECTURAL SIMULATION

<u>Crucially, the phallic phantasy hinges on an approximation of reality, yet imagining a different reality in which obstacles and prohibitions are overcome, if not simply sidestepped. Another critical difference from reality is that the phantasy approximates wish fulfillment in the relative safety of the phantasy.</u>

In "Creative Writers and Day-Dreaming," 1908, Freud links a symbolic aspect of daydreaming and creative writing in adulthood to wish fulfillment and phantasy in infancy. Just as the child has phantasies, so too the adult daydreams. In daydreams, the adult "creates a world of his own, or rather, rearranges things of his world in a new way 'which' pleases him", builds "castles in the air and day-dreams" (Freud, 1908b: 143-144, 147). Thus, a daydream or a phantasy "hovers...between 3 times...some provoking occasion in the present.... From there it harks back to a memory of an earlier experience (usually an infantile one)...and it now creates a situation relating to the future, which represents a fulfillment of the wish" (Freud, 1908b: 147). For a "'dreamer in broad daylight," past, present, and future are strung together, as it were, on the thread of the wish that runs through them (Freud, 1908b: 147,149).The creative writer helps his audience overcome unconscious resistances to the phantasy "by...disguising it, and he bribes us by the purely formal – that is, aesthetic – yield of pleasure he offers us in the presentation of his phantasies" (Freud, 1908b: 153).

Simulation, wishes, and world views

Like the phallic phantasy, architectural simulation often arises as an expression of wishful ideas about what ought to be rather than simply what is. As a result, simulation often expresses ideas about what is believed to be real and true for architecture, or ought to be real and true. Historically, in line drawings from Vitruvius to Libeskind's "Vertical Horizon," architectural simulation has expressed world views and cultural perspectives, particularly what is regarded as proper or real for architecture and simulation. If built work has served to materially substantiate and entrench a world view, architectural simulation has strategically supported daydreaming alternative world views.

Like the phallic phantasy, architectural simulation often arises as an expression of wishful ideas about what ought to be rather than simply what is. As a result, simulation often expresses ideas about what is believed to be real and true for architecture, or ought to be real and true.

To understand "Vertical Horizon" as an ideational representative of unconscious phallic impulses is to understand it as a challenge to obstacles to wish fulfillment. Style conventions can be perceived as obstacles to design wishes. Hence, conventions based on the idealization of closed form and the representation of the human body can be perceived as obstacles to the expression of open form and vice versa, as discussed in earlier chapters. Similarly, tradition generally holds that architectural design simulation e.g., the design drawing, outlines a proper building with proper part-to-whole relationships based on traditional ideals. Drawings that do not do this are not properly architectural. That convention runs from the ancient philosopher Plato's ruminations on the line and the simile in *The Republic*, c. 380 BC, through *De Architectura*, c. 30–15 BC by Vitruvius, to the Renaissance historian Giorgio Vasari's notion of design in *The Lives of the Most Excellent Painters, Sculptors, and Architects*, 1568, to *Architecture in the Age of Divided Representation*, 2004, by the architectural historian and theorist Dalibor Vesely. From a traditional perspective, "Vertical Horizon" is taboo in the sense that it does not outline a proper building for construction, and part-to-whole relationships in the drawing do not express traditional ideals.

"Vertical Horizon," in contrast, offers itself as a challenge to traditional simulation and traditional architecture, perhaps as a simulation of open form if not formless form.

To understand "Vertical Horizon" as an ideational representative of unconscious phallic impulses is to understand it as a challenge to obstacles to wish fulfillment.

"Vertical Horizon" is also situated amid other longstanding though nonetheless conflicting ideals, ideals that simulation has rather unagnostically supported. For example, line drawing was recruited in support of subjective beliefs as well as scientific principles in the Renaissance (Ackerman, 1998: 13), Renaissance ideals as well as Baroque ideals (Wölfflin, 1932: vii), Euclidian as well as non-Euclidean ideals, and "uncritical" photorealistic and imitative conventions as well as critical challenges to design conventions and orthodoxy (Eisenman, 1984: 212–227). "Vertical Horizon" appears to be subjective as well as systematic and technically precise. It combines rectilinear (i.e., Renaissance architectonic) as well as painterly (i.e., Baroque) elements, and it appears to combine Euclidian as well as non-Euclidean geometries. By combining these longstanding though nonetheless conflicting ideals in one drawing, "Vertical Horizon" utilizes simulation critically, not imitatively and uncritically, thus demonstrating the potential of simulation to call conventions and taboos into question. As Freud suggested in "Creative Writers and Day-Dreaming", like the "'dreamer in broad daylight,' past, present, and future are strung together…on the thread of the wish that runs through them (Freud, 1908b: 147,149). And perhaps, with "Vertical Horizon," Libeskind helps his audience overcome unconscious resistances to his architectural phantasy "by disguising it, and he bribes us by the purely formal – that is, aesthetic – yield of pleasure" the drawing offers (Freud, 1908b: 153).

Similarly, "Vertical Horizon" implicates itself in architecture versus not-architecture beliefs and taboos. For example, "Vertical Horizon" challenges the notion that the line and the diagram are instruments with which architecture imposes what is materially real and true for architecture as a physical construction on what is not architecture. Thus, "Vertical Horizon" appears to work against the notion that the critical function of architecture simulation is to force not-architecture systems of meaning or areas of knowledge to conform to the material requirements of architecture, ensuring that architecture does not naively and uncritically mold itself to that which is not-architecture (e.g., Allen, 1998: 16–1). "Vertical Horizon" appears to advance not-architecture as architecture, which, strictly speaking, is a taboo for those who believe architecture is or at least ought to be distinct and separate from other disciplines. Crucially, "Vertical Horizon" expresses the idea that architectural simulation is fundamentally different than the material requirements of architecture designed for construction. And in that way, the drawing suggests that what is critically at stake is something other than traditional ideals or conventional emphasis on building construction. Thus, there are a number of ways "Vertical Horizon" can be appreciated as an example of the role that critical simulation can play in challenging obstacles to wish fulfillment in the external world. "Vertical Horizon" challenges obstacles, prohibitions, and taboos partly by blurring distinctions between architectural imagination and reality and perceived obstacles.

"Vertical horizon" and the plot of phallic phantasy

As suggested earlier, to understand "Vertical Horizon" as an ideational representative of unconscious phallic impulses is to understand it as a challenge to obstacles to wish fulfillment. The discussion so far has helped clarify various kinds of obstacles to architectural wish fulfillment and how the drawing appears to challenge if not overcome the obstacles. It is also crucial to understand that "Vertical Horizon" can be experienced. For example, from Chapter 4, one can recall Moholy-Nagy's "space relationships" drawing, the plot of the drawing (closed form versus open form), and experiences associated with closed form and open form. Similarly, "Vertical Horizon" offers itself for experience, including an ideationally representative experience that approximates the plot of the phallic phantasy. That is because, like the plot of the phallic phantasy, "Vertical Horizon" represents the idea of overcoming prohibitions and taboos against having the object of affection in the way one wants it. In "Vertical Horizon," we can suppose that the object of affection is architecture. And as a drawing that can be experienced, like the phallic phantasy, "Vertical Horizon" affords the opportunity to experience the object virtually. Some details of that experience can be unpacked here.

In "Vertical Horizon," we can suppose the object of affection is architecture. And as drawing that can be experienced, like the phallic phantasy, "Vertical Horizon" affords the opportunity to experience the object virtually.

First, the title, "Vertical Horizon" signals that the spatiality of the drawing is oxymoronic, which is to say it has contradictory spatial qualities. A horizon, the title suggests, can be vertical. And perhaps the title suggests the vertical and horizontal axis of experience can be folded into one another, with the experience of the vertical axis of the building extruded up from land and the experience of the horizontal axis of the landscape extended to the horizon. Provocative implications flow from that basic premise, provocations that challenge architecture versus not-architecture conventions. One implication is that folding the vertical and horizontal axis together entails folding building and landscape together, thus suggesting a spatiality in which architecture is landscape and vice versa. Similarly, as a simulation of architecture, the drawing suggests that reality and phantasy can be folded into each other, whereby the architect can virtually have and virtually experience architecture. One can design and draw an imaginary world-of-one's-own and experience it virtually, even if only narcissistically. One could share the drawing with others, in which case one's imaginary world can be "liked" or not liked and can be judged by others as "proper" or not. Finally, "Vertical Horizon" suggests how architecture might fold the experiences of adulthood and childhood into each other. That is, through an ideational chain of associations and substitutions, a drawing can point to impulses that define selfhood and imagination in the phallic phase. In that sense, the drawing can be a place where the child-who-became-an-architect enjoys a special relationship with architectural objects, special partly because they are identified with prohibitions and taboos in the external world.

Crucially, and equally important to its status as a phallic object, critical simulation affords the opportunity to cast oneself in a phallic role, a role in which one has the object and experiences the object in the way one wants it. Like the phallic phantasy, critical architectural simulation can represent a phantasy of control and self-determination. As Freud's thought suggests, with critical simulation the architect "creates a world of his own, or rather, rearranges things of his world in a new way which pleases him" (Freud, 1908b: 143-144). The phantasy clings to reality insofar as it clings to an object of affection outside the phantasy. So too, "Vertical Horizon" presents so-called real architectonic elements: planar slabs, box forms, openings such as windows or doors, column shapes, beam shapes. Those features suggest that "Vertical Horizon" outlines real architecture, but the provocative arrangement of elements suggests it is also castles in the air. Yet one of the most systematic features of "Vertical Horizon" is that it lacks a consistent orthographic convention. Plan view, section view, elevation view, axonometric view, and perspective view appear to be combined in the drawing. The superimposition of elements in different views suggests depth of space, but overall it appears to be a shallow depth of space without light and shadow, all reinforcing its other-worldliness.

<u>Crucially, and equally important to its status as a phallic object, critical simulation affords the opportunity to cast oneself in a phallic role, a role in which one has the object and experiences the object in the way one wants it.</u>

Finally, like phallic phantasy, "Vertical Horizon" clings to reality but is a phase apart from reality. That critical difference sets the phantasy simulation apart from obstacles to satisfaction in the external world. Further still, the phantasy simulation is experienced in the present (one can see and experience the drawing in the present), but the phantasy simulation wishfully and longingly imagines what "ought" to be (depicting what one wants but cannot actually have). And, while looking forward, the phantasy simulation also unconsciously looks back, as in a rearview mirror, through a chain of ideational connections to repressed impulses in childhood. In those ways, critical architectural simulation can express the oxymoronic logic of the phallic phantasy and offer itself as an ideational representative of selfhood and self-determination in the phallic phase of childhood.

Conclusion

In this chapter, Freud's thought on the phallic phase in childhood helped explore the architectural empathy for simulation as a means to explore wishful ideas, particularly critical simulation that combines reality and phantasy to overcome prohibitions and taboos. Phallic phantasy is a defining aspect of selfhood and self-determination in the phallic phase, and like other phases it sets the stage for unconscious dispositions and associations in adulthood. In the phallic phantasy, the child casts itself in a phallic role, a role in which the child has its object of affection in the way that the child wants it. Phallic phantasy hinges on an approximation of reality, though a different reality, a critical difference in which obstacles and prohibitions against satisfaction are overcome. Thus, the phallic phantasy is also a phantasy of control and self-determination.

"Vertical Horizon" suggests how simulation affords the freedom to explore fanciful architectural ideas, ideas conflicting with conventional prohibitions and taboos in the external world. This chapter situated "Vertical Horizon" among longstanding though conflicting ideals regarding what is proper for architecture and architectural simulation, ideals that simulation has supported equally. Like the phallic phantasy, critical simulation calls into question perceived prohibitions and taboos against wish fulfillment. "Vertical Horizon" challenges conventional architectural prohibitions and taboos while offering a fanciful and virtual experience of architecture that clings to reality or "the real." One might identify with "Vertical Horizon" and find it to be compelling as a vaguely familiar though unconscious affirmation of selfhood and self-determination in the phallic phase. On the other hand, one might find it troubling, perhaps despicable, if unconsciously it is an unwelcome reminder of repressed phallic impulses. Finally, "Vertical Horizon" compares well with Freud's thought on the phallic phase, suggesting how phantasy and the real are overlapping categories of selfhood while calling into question conventional notions about what is real and true and proper for architectural simulation, design, and aesthetic experience.

CHAPTER 7

Spaces of social encounter: freedoms and constraints

Historically, a fundamental task for architecture has been to structure social relationships. Architects have long responded to that task by designing spaces for specific kinds of social interactions. In 1851, the architect Gottfried Semper suggested that task is so important that, along with the wall, floor, and roof, a social meeting area or social "hearth" space is one of the 4 fundamental elements of architecture (Semper, 1851: 102). Since then, many thinkers have considered how modern architecture arranges the elements of architecture to define social freedoms and constraints for specific kinds of social interaction. Freud's thought on the last phase of development in childhood, the genital phase, helps explain why the architect, and others, might have empathy for spaces of social encounter that separate, isolate, and formally configure social interactions, or the opposite as in the case of architect Rem Koolhaas' appreciation of undivided open areas intended to architecturally support emancipatory social interactions.

Freud's thought on the last phase of development in childhood…

helps explain why the architect, and others, might have empathy

for spaces of social encounter that separate, isolate, and formally

configure social interactions, or the opposite as in the case of…

appreciation of undivided open areas intended to architecturally

support emancipatory social interactions.

The Educatorium by Koolhaas/OMA, 1997, in Utrecht, The Netherlands, is a demonstrative example of how an architect can employ the elements of architecture to define social freedoms as well as constraints in its spaces of social encounter. The plan of the first floor, shown in Figure 7, the floor above the ground level, is illuminating. The plan shows the first floor as well as ground floor areas beyond. That is because there are large openings in the first floor that are open to the ground floor below. Also, parts of the first floor slope upward near the entrance and at lecture halls such that part of the cafeteria on the ground floor below the lecture halls is shown instead of the entire length of the lecture halls on the first floor. While those features of the design make the plan difficult to understand at first, they suggest how the building connects social spaces of encounter on upper and lower floors while also contrasting social freedoms and constraints on each floor. On the one hand, there are the institutional spaces of encounter, lecture halls and exam rooms, defined by walls that separate, isolate, and formally configure enclosed space for the types of institutional encounters within the rooms. Koolhaas regards those rooms as regime rooms, which is to say they are institutional rooms that represent how governments define and control social interaction. On the other hand, there are open social-mixer areas where there are few if any walls or corridors to separate or isolate or constrain social interactions among people inhabiting the spaces outside of the regime rooms. The open areas are intended to function socially as "open territories," for "rendezvous and exchange" and "inclusion," allowing "indeterminate configurations of inhabitation" where occupants may "drift" (Cornubert, 1998: 42–47). Further, Koolhaas explains, the open areas are intended as an "architecture of emancipation" that counterbalances the regime rooms that foster "social mimesis" (interview with Zaera-Polo, 1992: 27).

By pitching open social-mixer spaces in the Educatorium against enclosed regime rooms, Koolhaas established an important example of how architecture combines social freedoms and constraints to support different kinds of social interaction. Many thinkers view architecture and its spaces of encounter as effects of a social "will" of an era, which is a defining spirit and mood, also called the "zeitgeist" of an era. Many have suggested that the will of an era

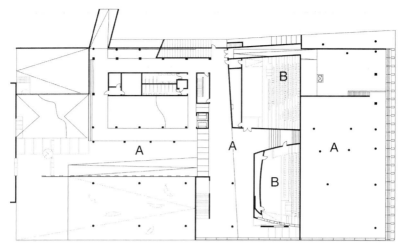

Figure 7 Educatorium, plan of first floor showing ground floor areas beyond, Rem Koolhaas/OMA, 1997, redrawn: open areas (A) versus regime rooms (B).

is decisively influenced by the technology of the era, also suggesting that, for better and for worse, modern architecture is an effect of a technological zeitgeist. The contrasting perspectives on modern architecture expressed by Camillo Sitte and Otto Wagner, outlined in Chapter 2, represent contrasting opinions on the social benefits and costs of the modern zeitgeist in Vienna at the turn of the 20th century.

<u>By pitching open social-mixer encounter spaces in the Educatorium against enclosed social encounter spaces, Koolhaas established an important example of how architecture combines social freedoms and constraints to support different kinds of social interaction.</u>

The presence or absence of walls suggests how modern architecture configures open or enclosed spaces of social encounter, and how architecture configures social freedoms and constraints in social relations. As in the case of the Educatorium, institutions (academic, corporate, legal, and health) and architecture combine to configure open or enclosed spaces for certain kinds of social encounter. Simultaneously, institutions combine with architecture to project the social power of the institutions into the public and private spheres of life, as many thinkers have noted (Tafuri, 1976. Foucault, 1977. Forty, 1992. Marcus, 1993.Evans, 1997. Duffy, 1998. Hughes and Sadler, 2000. Steele, 2005). While earlier chapters have explored the empathy for open form as well as empathy for closed form, this chapter builds on the earlier explorations by focusing on how architecture expresses the empathy for open-ended social encounters and, on the other hand, empathy for clearly defined and ordered social encounters. Freud's thought on the final phase of psychical development in childhood, the genital phase, helps explain the empathy for the one or the other space of social encounter and the freedoms and constraints suggested by each.

The last phase of development in childhood, the genital phase, and the search for obtainable objects

In *Three Essays*, 1905 (1920), Freud says the last phase of development in childhood, the genital phase, involves the transition to adulthood, whereby turning away from the unobtainable object in the phallic stage and associated prohibitions and taboos identified with the parents in that stage leads to the search for obtainable objects. Freud summed up the prohibitions and taboos that give rise to the phallic phantasy as oedipal constraints, or rather the "oedipal complex." In the genital stage, the child turns away from oedipal constraints and turns away from the special object of affection in the phallic phase to search for potentially obtainable objects with which to enjoy a sexual life as an adult, perhaps leading to parenthood. Turning away from oedipal constraints involves the repression of impulses and prohibitions associated with the parents, thus the repression of the oedipal complex. Repression in the genital phase has lasting implications and a defining influence on adult character (Freud, 1905 (1920): 207. 1912: 181).

...the last phase of development in childhood...involves the transition to adulthood, whereby turning away from the unobtainable object...and associated prohibitions and taboos...leads to the search for obtainable objects.

In *Three Essays*, 1905 (1920), "The Unconscious," 1915, and "Mourning and Melancholia," 1917, Freud notes that repression coincides with transitions from one phase of development to the next, as outlined in Chapter 4. Repression involves abandoning a special object in each phase in order to pass on to the next phase. Through repression, the abandoned object and sense of self in each phase become unconsciously linked and form the ego. Thus, each phase establishes a "demand made upon the mind for work" due to unique impulses in each phase (Freud, 1905 (1920): 168, 197–198. Freud, 1915c: 177–178. 1917a: 249).

The demands on the mind in the genital phase involve abandoning the oedipal complex in order to psychically navigate away from the oedipal home, which has become a kind of prison in the sense that the child is bounded by the oedipal framework under the watchful eye of the parents. The new emancipatory aim is to rid oneself of obstacles to new potentially obtainable objects. On the other hand, the child may unconsciously choose to hide from its impulses, directing attention away from them. For example, obsessive and compulsive behaviors express symbolic and ideational substitutions and displacements, diverting attention from impulses and potential contact with reminders of impulses, thus avoiding impulses (Freud, 1913: 324).

Similarly, adulthood obsessive and compulsive behaviors express unconscious wishes to contain repressed impulses and to psychically avoid or stave off possible reminders of the impulses. Thus, Freud said, obsessive and compulsive behaviors are ideational representatives of unconscious wishes that hark back through a chain of associations to impulses in the phases of development. Threshold practices first appearing in the anal phase are recruited in the genital phase for similar purposes, again expressing the unconscious wish to avoid reminders of troubling repressed impulses. Threshold practices (described in Chapter 5) involve preoccupations with establishing psychical and physical boundaries, divisions, or gaps in time or between objects, or decontamination rituals. Similarly, self-imposed and self-disciplinary prohibitions and taboos on touching can signify "removing the possibility of contact" (Freud, 1926: 122).

The case of "Little Hans," 1909, features prominently in Freud's observations on oedipal prohibitions and taboos. The case is perhaps Freud's most well-known example of oedipal anxieties that can lead to a spatial phobia (now generally known as agoraphobia). Agoraphobia inhibits the freedom to move about, particularly in public areas often simply called "public square" areas. In *Inhibitions, Symptoms, and Anxiety*, 1926, Freud returned to the case of "Little Hans" and summarized it succinctly. Briefly, inside Hans' home, Hans felt safe from the street. A chain of ideational substitutions led Hans to avoid the street. He avoided the street to avoid a horse. He avoided the horse because it might bite. Hans associated a horse bite with his father because Hans also feared his father might castrate him as punishment for his impulses and imagined transgressions toward his special object of affection, his mother. Thus, the case of "Little Hans" helps explain how architectural spaces of social encounter might be experienced as "safe" or "threatening" due to a chain of unconscious ideational associations. The street can become a space of encounter with troubling unconscious reminders about "dangerous" repressed impulses. Similarly, avoidance of public square areas may express unconscious associations leading back to oedipal prohibitions and impulses.

<u>...the street can become a space of encounter with troubling unconscious reminders about "dangerous" repressed impulses. Similarly, avoidance of public square areas may express unconscious associations....</u>

The genital phase brings about a unique transformation that sums up and rules over identifications in earlier phases. In *The Ego and the Id*, 1923, Freud notes that transformations in the genital phase are such that parts of the ego are cleaved off to form a kind of "preserve," the superego. The id is the part of the psyche that represents pleasure-seeking impulses in each phase of development. While the early identifications in each phase remain as parts of the ego, as ghosts of earlier epochs of selfhood, the rise of the superego represents a further repression of those identifications. The superego represents an identification with the parents, particularly the watchful eye of the parents, which the child associates with prohibitions against impulses in all phases. The superego overrules the earlier ego developments and impulses and keeps a watchful critical eye over them. Consequently, the superego is a substitute for the parents and becomes the locus of reaction formations that serve as defensive systems of thought such as morality, ideals, authoritative models, critical judgment, and persecutory agencies of watching and measuring, as well as obsessional and compulsive ideas and practices.

The id strives to indulge in impulses, and the superego defends against them. The ego now represents the external world as a "reality principle" that the ego associates with obstacles in the external world to the demands and critical judgments of the superego. The ego also attempts to satisfy the impulses of the id, impulses associated with a "pleasure principle," which must be balanced against the reality principle and the demands of the superego (Freud, 1923a: 25, 28–36, 53–54).

The way that superego transformations are resolved in childhood results in adult "character traits" that express a "disposition" or rather a prominence of one or another phase of development, though adult character traits express a mixture of dispositions (Freud, 1905(1920): 238–239). Freud suggested that even in view of the "infinite varieties" among all people, the main types of disposition appear to be 3 "libidinal types": erotic, narcissistic, and obsessional, but that the "mixed type" is more common (Freud, 1931: 217).

Notwithstanding the potential status of the architect as a special kind of leader, at least as cultivated and promoted by architects, it is perhaps not surprising that

Freud's observations on libidinal types among all people confirm what everyday experience suggests to also be fairly common traits of the architect. For example, the erotic type above all wishes to be loved and fears the loss of love, expresses the dominance of the id and its "elementary instinctual demands" (Freud, 1931: 217). Similarly, many architects desire praise, want to be loved for their gifts, and are anxious that their gifts might be rejected. Those traits echo selfhood and self-determination in the anal phase, as described in Chapter 5.

The narcissistic type is mainly concerned with self-preservation and loving as opposed to being loved, which expresses the dominance of the ego. They are "independent" and not "susceptible to intimidation." They are the "personalities," "leaders" who "give fresh stimulus to cultural development" and "damage the established state of affairs" (Freud, 1931: 218). Here, archetypal provocateurs come to mind, change agents, architects that challenge established rules and are loved and loathed for it. Narcissistic traits can echo selfhood and self-determination in the oral, anal, and phallic phases, as described in Chapters 4, 5, and 6.

The obsessional type is above all concerned with conscience and expresses the dominance of the superego. They are, Freud writes, "the true, pre-eminently conservative vehicles of civilization" (Freud, 1931: 218). Those traits suggest the architect who above all is concerned with ethics, adherence to rules, regulations, and following protocols, practice conventions, and guidelines. Those traits echo selfhood and self-determination closely identified with the ruling agencies of the superego arising in the genital phase, described in this chapter.

The idea that there are infinite varieties of character traits that combine to express the prominence of more than one phase of development is crucial. That idea helps explain why an architect, or others, might at one time or another express empathy that echoes selfhood and self-determination in more than one phase of development in childhood, if not in all phases. The same would be suggested by avoidance and reactions against potential reminders of one or more phase. The identifications with objects in the different phases remain in the adult psyche but are subordinate to the superego that rules over them. Repression and identification in each phase as well as adulthood dispositions that often define adult character types are normal (Freud, 1913: 323). They express the "innate constitutional roots of the sexual instinct" that are "innate in *everyone*" (Freud's italics), whereby "an unbroken chain bridges the gap between the neuroses in all their manifestations and normality" (Freud, 1905 (1920): 171).

The idea that there are infinite varieties of character traits that combine to express the prominence of more than one phase of development is crucial. That idea helps explain why an architect, or others, might at one time or another express empathy that echoes selfhood and self-determination in more than one phase of development in childhood, if not in all phases.

Open slab versus regime room: empathy for freedom versus constraint in spaces of social encounter

Freud's thought on the genital phase offers a compelling perspective on Koolhaas' empathy for architecture of emancipation. The Educatorium defines the architecture of emancipation in terms of open-slab social-mixer areas pitched against regime rooms. Parts of the building appear to express a wish, as Freud said, to "abolish all spatial barriers" between the ego and potentially obtainable objects in the space of social encounter. On the other hand, the enclosed regime rooms in the building express a wish to separate, isolate, and formally configure social interactions. The elements of architecture, e.g., the floor slab and wall, readily support either wish, suggesting that a social meeting area can be defined architecturally with either an open slab or enclosing walls. Both types of space could be spaces of social encounter. But programmatically, in terms of human activities in the Educatorium, the spaces express different aims for social encounter. One aim is for unstructured, open-ended, and indeterminate social encounters, and the other is for ordered, highly structured, and determinate social encounters. Ideationally, for Koolhaas, the one is emancipatory, open-ended to promote spontaneous social encounters. That kind of space is perhaps not an oedipal-regime space in the sense that it lends itself to turning away from the oedipal complex and the oedipal household. The other kind of space, the regime space, is constraining. It is defined by walls that separate and isolate and is defined by program-driven rules for social interaction. That kind of space harks back to the oedipal regime in so far as it serves to control occupants and positions occupants in hierarchically ordered social relationships. Those relationships direct attention to authority and disciplinary protocols of the institution (a school, a profession). The institutional aim is to project the protocols beyond the regime rooms of the institution into social life outside of the institution, life after classes.

Koolhaas' empathy for social-mixer spaces of encounter and the architecture of emancipation as opposed to social mimesis tally with Freud's thought on the "demand made upon the mind for work" in the last phase of development in childhood. Emancipation from the oedipal regime requires one to "abolish all spatial barriers" between the ego and new potentially obtainable objects. Koolhaas configures ramps, stairs, and entries to channel circulation flows to open social-mixer areas to foster spontaneous social encounters, and floor openings offer diagonal views for visual connectivity between floors, reinforcing visual and social connectivity. In contrast, Freud suggests, is self-isolation, like "Little Hans," who avoided the public street.

...empathy for social-mixer spaces of encounter and the architecture of emancipation as opposed to social mimesis tally with Freud's thought on the "demand made upon the mind for work" in the last phase of development in childhood.

The regime rooms of the Educatorium lend themselves to comparison with the agencies of the superego: authority and disciplinary protocols, ideals based on the parental models, persecutory watching and measuring and critical judgments, and threshold practices. Logically, the examination rooms, lecture halls, and administrative offices offer themselves as ideational representatives of the agencies of the superego. All serve the watchful authority, thresholds isolate occupants and types of activities, and interactions are governed by narrowly defined programmatic aims (lecture, examine, discipline, offer incentives and implied threats, administer praise, or punish). Empathy for, or personal identification with, regime rooms suggests a prominent identification with the watchful agencies of the superego. In that case, thresholds that formally segregate different types of social activity and architecturally signpost the types of interactions that are to be expected might be comforting. That kind of space is well caricatured in the office-cubicles-scene in the film "Playtime," 1967, by Jacques Tati (with architect Eugène Roman). However, in that scene, the affable but awkwardly traditional main character, Monsieur Hulot, finds the experience to be bewildering. Unlike other occupants depicted in the scene, Hulot does not seem comfortable in the space. Similarly, the film features other spaces of social encounter to suggest modern architecture is alienating.

While the Educatorium is a compelling example of how architecture expresses social freedoms and constraints in its spaces of social encounter, there are other examples. Not many, however, combine and contrast freedoms and constraints so explicitly.

The NTR Headquarters building by MVRDV, 1994–1997, and next door, the Villa VPRO, also by MVRDV, 1993–1997, in Hilversum, The Netherlands, are contrasting examples. Each suggests a contrasting client preference for workplace social encounters. As originally built, the NTR Headquarters emphasizes threshold strategies. The entry is a case in point. Entry into the building is gained by walking from the street sidewalk to the rooftop of the building, which is at the level of the sidewalk. Proceeding on the roof to an exterior stair leading down into a void in the building, the stair leads one to a landing where one gains entry into the building. Beyond the landing in the void, the building hovers above its sloped site. On the landing, one is physically and visually isolated from the interior of the building. Inside the entry door, a corridor with full-height partitions appears to join a series of offices with doors. Thus, the design offers itself as an example of threshold and isolation strategies. And though the building is part of a corporate office park or campus, it lacks a public lobby or gathering area that suggests it actually is part of a campus or a social network beyond the building.

On the other hand, the Villa VPRO office building, near the NTR building, provides a number of social areas lending themselves to open-ended social encounters. The social areas are strategically distributed throughout the building, establishing a labyrinth-like network of open areas for social encounter. In those areas, floor openings afford diagonal views in support of visual connectivity between floors, though generally the scale of each area is much less grand than those of the Educatorium. The degree of spatial segmentation in Villa VPRO is between that of the NTR building and the Educatorium. However, the degree of spontaneity in the spatial configurations of VPRO exceeds that of the Educatorium. That is perhaps not surprising. The original aim for VPRO was to relocate from the separate villa spaces the VPRO had been operating in to new headquarters that somehow retained the intimacy and improvisational social configurations of the former villa spaces, thus the name Villa VPRO. The affable and traditional Monsieur Hulot, having lived happily in a haphazard old apartment villa ("Mon Oncle," 1958, Tati), would perhaps have appreciated Villa VPRO.

Conclusion

This chapter drew from Freud to explore the empathy for spaces of social encounter defined on the one hand by freedoms and on the other hand by constraints. Historically, a fundamental task for architecture has been to structure social relationships. Many thinkers have considered how modern architecture arranges the elements of architecture to define social freedoms and constraints for specific kinds of social interaction. Freud's thought on the last phase of development in childhood, the genital phase, helps explain why the architect and others might have empathy for spaces of social encounter that separate, isolate, and formally configure social interactions. And Freud helps explain the empathy for the opposite as in the case of architect Rem Koolhaas' appreciation of undivided open areas intended to architecturally support emancipatory social interactions. In *Three Essays*, 1905 (1920), Freud indicates that the last phase of development involves the transition to adulthood, whereby one turns away from oedipal constraints identified with the parents and searches for obtainable objects, perhaps turning toward the public square. That compares well with empathy for the social-mixer areas of the Educatorium and the configuration of ramps, stairs, and entries that serve to channel people into the social-mixer areas to foster spontaneous social encounters. In contrast, the regime rooms of the Educatorium lend themselves to comparison with the agencies of the superego: adoption of authoritative models and ideals based on the parental models, persecutory watching and measuring and critical judgments, threshold practices and reaction formations, and other agencies of the superego. Though the project required regime rooms, Koolhaas' sought to counterbalance them with emancipatory spaces of social encounter.

Conclusion

The phases of psychical development in childhood are structural, Freud explained, and everyone passes through them. Adult experience and associated preferences, preoccupations, and motivations, Freud also explained, can be tell-tale signs that hark back through a psychical and symbolic chain of associations to the phases of development. The implications for the understanding of architectural experience are extensive. For example, the empathy for closed-form architecture, and on the other hand open-form, may be traceable through a chain of associations to developmental experiences in childhood.

Among the many examples of empathy for closed-form or open-form architecture that could be examined through the lens of Freud's thought on the psychical developments of childhood, some more clearly offer themselves as representative examples than others. Thus, Freud helps explain why open areas where people can freely associate and mix socially, like the social mixer areas of the Educatorium, designed by architect Rem Koolhaas, might be experienced unconsciously by some as pleasurable and vaguely familiar affirmations of selfhood and self-determination in the last stage of childhood. That insight is transferable to other comparable examples, such as the public square or street or shopping arcade.

On the other hand, depending on individual character type, social mixer areas might be experienced unconsciously by others as unwelcome reminders of repressed childhood impulses and phantasies. In such cases, the architectural setting challenges anxiety-avoidance strategies intended to distance oneself physically and ideationally from contact with reminders of repressed impulses and phantasies.

In a similar way, "social distancing" may present a psychical challenge for those who enjoy social mixing. Their unconscious experience of social distancing may be one of being caught in a ideational zone of representation where something is not there but should be.

In such cases, the experience of closed form or open form, or the preference for social mixing or social distancing, Freud's thought suggests that what may be at stake is a kind of drama, a mise-en-scène, that implicates architecture in the "projection of…the psychical apparatus" (Freud, SE XXIII, 300).

Bringing into focus Freud's thought on the phases of development in childhood has helped explain how the psychical agencies of selfhood and self-determination in childhood might shape adult architectural preferences and preoccupations.

Freud's thought suggests that the empathy for various types of architectural expression, e.g., closed form and open form, harks back through a psychical and symbolic chain of associations to the phases of development in childhood. And looking at the associations the other way around, each phase can be expected to contribute to architectural preferences and preoccupation, those of the child-who-became-an architect and any others as well.

The Educatorium and Villa VPRO (discussed in Chapter 7) are early examples of a recent trend to configure institutional and corporate work places as communication-and-social-exchange-places that promote social connectivity, group intelligence, open sourcing, and open-ended self-organization of work groups. A number of architectural thinkers have speculated on the implications for architecture and social organization (for examples, see *Corporate Fields*, ed., B. Steel (ed.), 2005; *Introduction to Collective Intelligence in Design, AD*, C. Hight, P. Morel, 2006; *The Organization and Architecture of Innovation*, T. Allen, G, Henn, 2007; *The Autopoiesis of Architecture I & II*, P. Schumacher, 2011, 2012). Most agree that the trend introduces new social media information technologies whose digital and virtual spaces exist a phase apart from physical architecture. Wireless connectivity and massive information flows augment and intensify social connectivity. Increasingly, social media and computational design technologies combine to influence how architecture configures social space, how it aims to optimize human interactions there, and how architecture expresses human, social, and architectural relationships.

What is perhaps less clear about the trend is how it may intensify the experience of psychical freedoms and constraints in spaces of social encounter. One likely possibility is to blur the distinction between the type of social space in the Educatorium defined as the regime room and the other type defined as the open-ended social mixer area. Communication-and-social-exchange spaces of encounter augmented by new media might be experienced by some as unconscious affirmations of selfhood and self-determination in childhood. On the other hand, the psychical experience may be one of being "caught...in a zone of representation" where one feels something "is there and should not be" (Cousins 1994: 63). In both cases, what is at stake is a kind of drama that implicates architecture as well as ideology and politics in the "projection of...the psychical apparatus" (Freud, SE XXIII, 300).

Further reading

The main chapters of this book call attention to thinkers in architecture (architects and theorists) who have explored how Freud can contribute to the understanding of architecture. Considering writings that further explore or broaden the psychoanalytic and architectural contexts for some of the concepts in *Freud for Architects*, additional reading might begin with *Psychoanalysis and Space* 2008, Martin and Holm, (eds.), particularly the chapter titled "Architectural Space-Form-Empathy Shadows the Unconscious", by the author. Similarly, additional reading might include "That 'oceanic feeling': Architectural Formlessness, Otherness, and Being Everything", and "Architectural Envelopment and the Late Avante-garde: The New, Critical Mimesis, and Indentification" also by the author, in *With Silence Implying Sound,* 2010, Pavlovits (ed.). Moreover, *Translation and the Nature of Philosophy*, 1989 (2014), by Andrew Benjamin, the philosopher and architecture theorist, explores how being and becoming are represented in avant-garde works. Benjamin draws from one of Freud's early papers on the deferred effects of repression (Nachträglichkeit) to explain the representation of being and becoming in particular works.

If considering Freud's successors (e.g., Klien, Winnicot, Lacan, Guattari), further reading might also include *The Architecture of Psychoanalysis*, 2017, by Jane Rendell, architect and theorist. Rendell draws on psychoanalytic concepts, some originating with Freud, to explore examples of how architectural settings and spatial attributes of psychical experience overlay one another.

Brunelleschi, Lacan, Le Corbusier, 2010, by Lorens Holm, architect and theorist, offers a compelling comparison of the Renaissance architect Filippo Brunelleschi's influential diagram explaining perspective and Jacques Lacan's influential diagram explaining the optical structure of desire. Lacan (1901–1981) was a leading psychoanalyst who believed himself to be the true heir to Freud, though Lacan's writings are dense, with enigmatic allusions to Freud's ideas. Holm also draws from Lacan to interpret a kind of pilgrimage to the Parthenon in Greece by the well-known modern architect Le Corbusier.

In *Architecture's Desire*, 2010, architecture theorist Michael Hays draws from Lacan's thought on the symbolic representation of the "real" and the "imaginary" to examine the architectural avant-garde in the 1970s. Hays explains the avant-garde as a system of representation and perception and identity grappling indirectly with what Lacan described as an inevitable and unrecoverable loss in childhood.

Further reading on open form and formlessness in the arts would do well to include *Formless: A User's Guide*, by Rosalind Krauss and Yve-Alain Bois, 1997, particularly the exploration of examples of material practices that negate form by means of "antiform" techniques, drawn in part from Lacan's ideas on acquiring a self-image in childhood to explain such work.

Other notable readings that bridge psychoanalytic ideas and architecture that can only be mentioned here are *Architecture and the Unconscious*, 2017, John Shannon Hendrix and Lorens Holm (eds.); *Sexuality & Space*, 1992, Beatriz Colomina (ed.); *Architecture and Psychoanalysis: Peter Eisenman and Jacques Lacan*, 2006, John Shannon Hendrix; and *Architecture for a Free Subjectivity*, 2011, Simone Brott.

References

Ackerman, J 1998, *The Reinvention of Architectural Drawing 1250–1550*, Sir John Soane Museum, London.

Allen, S 1998, "Diagrams Matter," (eds.) Ben van Berkel & Caroline Bos, "Diagram Work: Data Mechanics for a Topological Age" *Any, 23*, Anyone Corporation, New York.

Bachelard, G 1969, *The Poetics of Space*, (transl.) Maria Jolas, Beacon Press, Boston.

Beard, G 1869, *Our Home Physician*, E. B. Treat & Co, New York.

Boesiger, W 1995, *Le Corbusier Oeuvre Complete*, Birkhäuser, Basel.

Bramble, R M 2019, "Traumatic Consequences for Immigrant Populations in the United States," (ed.) B X Lee, *The Dangerous Case of Donald Trump*, Thomas Dunne Books, New York.

Coiffi, F 1998, *Freud and the Question of Pseudoscience*, Carus Publishing Company, Peru, Illinois.

Colomina, B 1988, "L'Esprit Nouveau: Architecture and Publicité," (ed.) *Architectureproduction*, Beatriz Colomina, Princeton Architectural Press, New York.

Cooper, A 2018, "Stormy Daniels describes her alleged affair with Donald Trump". 60 Minutes, 25 March.

Cornubert, C 1998, "Educatorium, Utrecht, Holland," Domus 800, January, 42–47, Milan.

Cousins, M 1996, 'Where?,' (eds.) Duncan McCoruodale, Katarina Ruedi & Sarah Wiggelsworth, *Desiring Practices*, Black Dog Publishing Ltd., London.

Cousins, M, and Hussain A 1984, *Michel Foucault*, Macmillan Ltd., London.

Cousins, M 1994, "The Ugly," *AA Files*, (28):61–64.

Cousins, M 2005, "The Aeffect," *Corporate Fields: Office Projects by the D[R]L Design Lab*, AA Publications, London.

Crews, F 2017, *Freud: The Making of an Illusion*, Metropolitan Books, New York.

Damousi, J and Plotkin, M 2009, *The Transnational Unconscious*, Palgrave Macmillan, Macmillan Publisher Ltd., Hampshire.

Danto, E 2005, *Freud's Free Clinics: Psychoanalysis and Social Justice, 1918–1938*. Columbia University Press, New York.

Danto, E 2009, "Three Roads from Vienna: Psychoanalysis, Modernism and Social Welfare." (eds.) Joy Damousi and Mariano Ben Plotkin, *The Transnational Unconscious*, Palgrave Macmillan, Macmillan Publisher Ltd., Hampshire.

Duffy, F, Jaunzens, D, Laing, A, and Willis, S 1998, *New Environments for Working*, Francis & Taylor, New York.

Eisenman, P 1984 (1996) "The End of the Classical: The End of the Beginning, the End of the End," (ed.) *The Yale Architecture Journal* 21, Reprint, *Theorizing a New Agenda for Architecture*, Kate Nesbitt, Princeton Architectural Press, New York.

Eisenman, P 1992, "Visions Unfolding," *Domus*, no. 734, 17–21, Rozzano.

Eisenman, P 1999, *Peter Eisenman Diagram Diaries*, Thames and Hudson, London.

Eisenman, P 2003, "Blurred Zones," Monacelli Press Inc., New York.

Evans, R 1997, *Translations from Drawing to Building and Other Essays*, The Architectural Association, London.

Forty, A 1992, *Objects of Desire*, Thames & Hudson, London.

Foucault, M 1967 (1984), "Of Other Spaces: Utopias and Heterotopias,"(transl.) Jay Miskowie, Architecture, Mouvement, Continuité, no. 5 (October 1984): 46–49; in Diacritics 16, no. 1 (Spring, 1986): 22–27.

Foucault, M 1977 (1995), *Discipline and Punish*, (transl.) Alan Sheridan, Vintage Books, New York.

Freud, S 1895, *Studies on Hysteria*, (eds.) The Standard Edition of the Complete Psychological Works of Sigmund Freud, (hereafter referred to as SE) SE II, (transl. eds.) James Stratchey and Anna Freud, The Hogarth Press, London.

Freud, S 1897, "The Architecture of Hysteria" SE I, (transl. eds.) James Stratchey in collaboration with Anna Freud, The Hogarth Press, London.

Freud, S 1900, *The Interpretation of Dreams* (eds.) The Standard Edition of the Complete Psychological Works of Sigmund Freud, SE IV, (transl. eds.) James Stratchey and Anna Freud, The Hogarth Press, London.

Freud, S 1901, *The Psychopathology of Everyday Life*, SE VI, (transl. eds.) James Stratchey in collaboration with Anna Freud, The Hogarth Press, London.

Freud, S 1905 (1920), "Three Essays on the Theory of Sexuality," SE VII, (transl. eds.) James Stratchey in collaboration with Anna Freud, The Hogarth Press, London.

Freud, S 1905, *Jokes and Their Relation to the Unconscious*, SE VIII, (transl. eds.) James Stratchey in collaboration with Anna Freud, The Hogarth Press, London.

Freud, S 1908a, "Character and Anal Eroticism," SE IX, (eds.) James Stratchey in collaboration with Anna Freud, The Hogarth Press, London.

Freud, S 1908b, Creative Writers and Day-Dreaming, SE IX, (eds.) James Stratchey in collaboration with Anna Freud, The Hogarth Press, London.

Freud, S 1910, "Wild Analysis," SE X, (transl. eds.) James Stratchey in collaboration with Anna Freud, The Hogarth Press, London.

Freud, S 1912, "The Tendency to Debasement in Love," SE XI, (transl. eds.) James Stratchey in collaboration with Anna Freud, The Hogarth Press, London.

Freud, S 1913, "The Disposition to Obsessional Neuroses," SE XII, SE XI, (transl. eds.) James Stratchey in collaboration with Anna Freud, The Hogarth Press, London.

Freud, S 1914, "Remembering Repeating and Working-Through," SE XII, (transl. eds.) James Stratchey in collaboration with Anna Freud, The Hogarth Press, London.

Freud, S 1915a, "Instincts and Their Vicissitudes," SE XIV, (transl. eds.) James Stratchey in collaboration with Anna Freud, The Hogarth Press, London.

Freud, S 1915b, "Repression," SE XIV, (transl. eds.) James Stratchey in collaboration with Anna Freud, The Hogarth Press, London.

Freud, S 1915c, "The Unconscious," SE XIV, (transl. eds.) James Stratchey in collaboration with Anna Freud, The Hogarth Press, London.

Freud, S 1916–1917, *Introductory Lectures on Psychoanalysis*, SE XIV, (transl. eds.) James Stratchey in collaboration with Anna Freud, The Hogarth Press, London.

Freud, S 1917a, "Mourning and Melancholia," SE XIV, (transl. eds.) James Stratchey in collaboration with Anna Freud, The Hogarth Press, London.

Freud, S 1917b, "On Transformations of Instinct as Exemplified in Anal Eroticism," SE XVII, (transl. eds.) James Stratchey in collaboration with Anna Freud, The Hogarth Press, London.

Freud, S 1920, "Beyond the Pleasure Principle," SE XVIII, (transl. eds.) James Stratchey in collaboration with Anna Freud, The Hogarth Press, London.

Freud, S 1923a, "The Ego and the Id," SE XIX, (transl. eds.) James Stratchey in collaboration with Anna Freud, The Hogarth Press, London.

Freud, S 1923b, "The Infantile Genital Organization" SE XIX, (transl. eds.) James Stratchey in collaboration with Anna Freud, The Hogarth Press, London.

Freud, S 1924, "Dissolution of the Oedipus Complex", SE XIX, (transl. eds.) James Stratchey in collaboration with Anna Freud, The Hogarth Press, London.

Freud, S 1926, "Inhibition, Symptoms and Anxiety," SE XX, (transl. eds.) James Stratchey in collaboration with Anna Freud, The Hogarth Press, London.

Freud, S 1930, *Civilization and Its Discontents*, SE XXI, (transl. eds.) James Stratchey in collaboration with Anna Freud, The Hogarth Press, London.

Freud, S 1931, "Libidinal Types," XXI, (transl. eds.) James Stratchey in collaboration with Anna Freud, The Hogarth Press, London.

Freud, S 1941, "Findings, Ideas, Problems," SE XXIII, (transl. eds.) James Stratchey in collaboration with Anna Freud, The Hogarth Press, London.

Freud, S 1940, "An Outline of Psychoanalysis," SE XXIII, (transl. eds.) James Stratchey in collaboration with Anna Freud, The Hogarth Press, London.

Gay, P 1988, "Freud: A Life for Our Times," W.W. Norton & Company, Inc., New York.

Gay, P 1989, "*The Freud Reader*," W. W. Norton & Company, Inc, New York, N.Y.

Gay, P, Evans, J, and Redman, P 2000, "*Identity: A Reader*," SAGE and The Open University, London.

Giedion, S 1928 (1995), "*Building in France, Building in Iron Building in Ferroconcrete*," (transl.) J. Duncan Berry, The Getty Center for the History of Art and the Humanities, Santa Monica, CA.

Giedion, S 1941 (2003), "*Space, Time and Architecture: The Growth of a New Tradition*," 5th edition, Harvard University Press, Cambridge, MA.

Grosskurth, P 1991, "*The Secret Ring: Freud's Inner Circle and the Politics of Psychoanalysis*," Dianne Publishing Co, Darby, PA.

Herman, J 1992, "*Trauma and Recovery*," Basic Books, New York.

Hight, C, and Morel, P 2006, "Introduction to Collective Intelligence in Design," AD, #30, Wiley, Hoboken, NJ.

Holmes, L 2012, "Perversion and Pathology: a Critique of Psychoanalytic Criticism in art," *Journal of Aesthetic and Culture*, Vol. 4.

Hughes, J and Sadler, S 2000, "*Non-Plan Plan,*" Taylor & Francis, Oxon.

Husserl, E 1970, "*The Origin of Geometry*," (transl.) David Carr, Northwestern University Press, Evanston, IL.

Kandel, E 2012, "*The Age of Insight: the Quest to Understand the Unconscious in Art, Mind, and Brain, from Vienna 1900 to the Present*," Random House, New York.

Klein, M 1929 (1948), "Infantile Anxiety Situations Reflected in a Work of Art and the Creative Impulse," *Love, Guilt, and Reparation, and Other Works 1921–45*, The Hogarth Press, London.

Klein, M 1935 (1948), "A Contribution to the Psychogenesis of Manic-Depressive States," *Love, Guilt, and Reparation, and Other Works 1921–45*, The Hogarth Press, London.

Koch, A, Schwennsen, K, Dutton, T and Smith, D 2002, "*The Redesign of Studio Culture*," American Institute of Architecture Students, Inc, Washington, DC.

Koolhaas, R 1978, "Dali and Le Corbusier, the Paranoid Critical Method," *Architectural Design*, Vol. 2–3, London.

Koolhaas, R 1991, "New York/La Villette," *OMA/Rem Koolhaas*, Princeton Architectural Press, New York.

Lavin, S 2004, "*Form Follows Libido*," The MIT Press, Cambridge.

Lee, B 2019, "*The Dangerous Case of Donald Trump*," Thomas Dunne Books, New York.

Mallgrave, H F and Ikonomou, E 1994, "*Empathy, Form and Space*," (transl.) Harry Francis Mallgrave and Eleftherios Ikonomou, The Getty Center, Santa Monica, California.

Malgrave, H 2010, "*The Architect's Brain*," John Wiley & Sons Ltd, West Sussex.

Marks, S 2017, "Psychotherapy in Historical Perspective" *History of the Human Sciences*, Vol. 30(2): 3–16.

Marks, S 2018, "Psychotherapy in Europe," *History of the Human Sciences*, Vol. 31(4): 3–12.

Marcus, T 1993, "*Buildings and Power*," Routledge, New York.

Moholy-Nagy, L 1928(1947), "*The New Vision and Abstract of an Artist*," George Wittenborn Inc., New York.

National Architectural Accrediting Board, 2014, "2014 Condition for Accreditation," National Architectural Accrediting Board, Inc., Washington, DC.

Piñero, J L 1989, *Historical Origins of the Concept of Neuroses*," Cambridge University Press, Cambridge.

Phillips, A 2006, *Modern Classics Penguin Freud Reader*," Penguin Books Limited, London.

Pols, H, and Oak, S 2007, "War & Military Mental Health: the US Psychiatric Response in the 20th Century." *American Journal of Public Health*, Vol. 97: 12.

Rowe, C, and Slutzky, R 1963, "Transparency: Literal and Phenomenal" *Perspecta*, Vol. 8: 45–54.

Schmarsow, A 1893 (1994), "The Essence of Architectural Creation," *Empathy, Form and Space*, (transl.) Harry Francis Mallgrave and Eleftherios Ikonomou, The Getty Center for the History of Art and the Humanities, Santa Monica, CA.

Schorske, C 1980, "*Fin De Siècle Vienna: Politics and Culture*," Alfred A. Knopf, Inc., New York.

Segal, H 1952, "A Psycho-Analytic Approach to Aesthetics," *The International Journal of Psychoanalysis*, Vol. 33: 196–207.

Semper, G 1851 (1989), "*The Four Fundamental Elements of Architecture*," *Gottfried Semper, The Four Fundamental Elements of Architecture and Other Writings*, (transl.) Harry Francis Mallgrave and Wolfgang Herrmann, Cambridge University Press, Cambridge.

Semper, G 1860 (1989), "*Style in the Technical and Tectonic Arts*," (eds.) Francis Mallgrave, Wolfgang Herrmann, and Gottfried Semper, Cambridge University Press, Cambridge, MA.

Steele, B 2005, *Corporate Fields*, (ed.) The Architectural Association, London.

Stratchey J and Freud A, 1966, "Notes on Some Technical Terms," SE I, (transl. eds.) James Stratchey in collaboration with Anna Freud, The Hogarth Press, London.

Stokes, A 1932 (1968), "*The Quattro Cento*," Schoken Books, New York.

Stokes, A 1934 (1969), "*Stones of Rimini*," Schoken Books, New York.

Tafuri, M 1976 (1999), "*Architecture and Utopia*," MIT Press, Cambridge, MA.

Tschumi, B 1975, "*Advertisements for Architecture*." Bernard Tschumi Architects, www.tschumi.com/projects/19/.

Vidler, A 1990 (1996), "Theorizing the Unhomely," *Theorizing a New Agenda for Architecture*, (ed.) Kate Nesbitt, Princeton Architectural Press, New York.

Vidler, A 1992, *The Architectural Uncanny*, MIT Press, Cambridge, MA.

Vidler, A 1994, "The Psychopathologies of Modern Space: Metropolitan Fear from Agoraphobia to Estrangement," *Rediscovering History*, (ed.) Michael S. Roth, Stanford University Press, Stanford, CA.

Vidler, A 2000, *Warped Space*, MIT Press, Cambridge, MA.

Vischer, R 1873 (1994), "On the Optical Sense of Form: A Contribution to Aesthetics," (transl) Harry Francis Mallgrave and Eleftherios Ikonomou, *Empathy, Form and Space*, The Getty Center, Santa Monica, CA.

Volker, W 2011, "*Ernst L. Freud, Architect: The Case of the Modern Bourgeois Home*," Berghahn Books, New York.

Weston, D 2002, "Implications of Developments in Cognitive Neuroscience for Psychoanalytic Psychotherapy," *Harvard Review of Psychiatry*, Vol. 10(6): 369–73.

Wölfflin, H 1886 (1994), "*Prolegomena to a Psychology of Architecture*," (eds.) Harry Francis Mallgrave and Eleftherios Ikonomou, *Empathy, Form and Space*, The Getty Center for the History of Art and the Humanities, Santa Monica, CA.

Wölfflin, H 1915 (1929), "*Principles of Art History*," (transl.) M.D. Hottinger, G. Bell & Sons, Dover Publications, Mineola, NY.

Zaretsky, E 2004, "*Secrets of the Soul*," Vintage Books, New York.

Zaretsky, E 2009, "Beyond the Blues: Richard Wright, Psychoanalysis, and the Modern Idea of Culture," *The Transnational Unconscious*, (eds.) Joy Damousi & Mariano Ben Plotkin, Palgrave Macmillan, Macmillan Publisher Ltd., Hampshire.

Zaretsky, E 2015, "*Political Freud: A History*," Columbia University Press, New York.

Zaera-Polo, A 1992, "Finding Freedoms: Conversations With Rem Koolhaas," El Croquis, Madrid, Vol. 53: 6–31.

Index

Note: Italicized pages refer to figures.

adults/adulthood 3; anal character traits 70; object relations 61–62; obsessive and compulsive behaviors 96; psychical helplessness 32; sexual experience 21

aeffects 12, 13

aesthetic experience/intuition 37–53; Giedion's ideas about 42–43; internal motives and 39; Klein's idea of reparation for 45–46, 47; Moholy-Nagy's ideas about 43–44; Neutra's design thinking 48–50; Schmarsow's ideas about 40–41, 43–44; Semper's ideas about 37, 38–39, 41; Stokes's ideas about 44–47; theorists and designers 37–38; Vischer's ideas about 40, 43; Wölfflin's ideas about 41–42, 43

affirmation of traumatic experience 32, 35

agoraphobia 19, 20, 52, 97

American Institute of Architecture Students (AIAS) 32

American Psychiatric Association 31

anal phase of development 15, 58, 68–72; impulses 68, 69, 71, 72; object 69–70; repression 71; self-centered pleasure 69; threshold practices 71–72; *see also* House II (Eisenman)

"Anna O" 30

"Anxiety and Instinctual Life" (Freud) 32

anxiety-avoidance strategies 105

The Architect's Brain (Mallgrave) 9

architectural gift *see* gift

The Architectural Uncanny (Vidler) 52

architecture: anthropomorphic model of 52; creative production of 39; Freud's thought 5–6; nontraditional designs 52; psychoanalytic theory 6; *see also* aesthetic experience/intuition

Architecture in the Age of Divided Representation (Vesely) 85

"The Architecture of Hysteria" (Freud) 14, 27–28, *28*

Architecture of Hysteria" diagram (Freud) 14

architecture schools 5–6

art 44–47; *see also* aesthetic experience/intuition

artistic disposition 71

avant-garde designs 5

Baudelaire, Charles 26–27

Berneys, Martha 23

Beyond the Pleasure Principle (Freud) 57–58

birth trauma 48, 49

blurred zones 15, 51, 62–66; *see also* Rebstockpark masterplan (Eisenman)

Blurred Zones (Eisenman) 51

body experience 2

brain 9

breast, as an object 60

Breuer, Josef 25–26

building design 5

Building in France (Giedion) 42–43

Calvinist Reformed Church 21

carving 46

categorical thinking strategies 72

Character Analysis (Reich) 48

"Character and Anal Eroticism" (Freud) 61

character traits 98–100; dispositions 98–100; erotic 98; infinite varieties 98, 99–100; libidinal 98, 99; narcissistic 98, 99; obsessional 98, 99

Charcot, Jean-Martin 26–27

child/childhood: developmental experiences 21; memories 2–3; oxymoronic circumstances 64; phallic phantasy 16; phallic role 81; self-centered pleasure 69; self-image 60; sensory organs 21; unconscious wishes 21–22; *see also* phases of psychical development

"Childhood Memories and Screen Memories" (Freud) 28–29

Chuey House (Neutra) 48, 49

City Building (Sitte) 19

Civilization and its Discontents (Freud) 8

"A Clinical Lesson at the Salpêtrière" (Brouillet) 26

clinical practices 8

closed form 4, 37, 68–78, 105, 106; architectural conception of 73; empathy for 73; House II (Eisenman) 68, *69*, 75–78; human body as 73; rule-based composition 72–78

collective unconscious 35

Colomina, Beatriz 74–75

combat trauma *see* shell shock

consumer preferences 5

Cousins, Mark 12

Creative Writers and Daydreaming (Freud) 8

"Creative Writers and Day-Dreaming" (Freud) 8, 84, 86

creative writing 84

Crews, Frederick 23

critical simulation *see* simulation

Cullen, William 26

"Dali and Le Corbusier, the Paranoid Critical Method" (Koolhaas/ OMA) 50

daydreams/daydreaming 2–3, 84; symbolic aspect of 84

De Architectura (Vitruvius) 74, 85

decontamination 76; *see also* ideational representatives

Delirious New York (Koolhaas) 11

Delueze, Gilles 66

depressive position 45

design *see* drawing/design

design studio 25

developmental experiences and
behaviors 21

developmental phases *see* phases
of psychical development

*Diagnostic and Statistical Manual of
Mental Disorders, Fourth Edition
(DSM-IV)* 31

*Diagnostic and Statistical Manual of
Mental Disorders, Third Edition
(DSM-III)* 31

dispositions 21, 60; artistic 71, 77;
character traits 98–100

"Dora" case 23

drawing/design 5; composition
72–75; Educatorium (Koolhaas/
OMA) 93–95, *94*, 100–102; House II
(Eisenman) 68, *69*, 76–77; Moholy-
Nagy's space relationships 15,
44, 54, *55*, 55–57, 63, 87; open-
corner designs 10; orthographic
conventions 79, 89; Rebstockpark
masterplan (Eisenman) 51, 62–66;
"Vertical Horizon" (Libeskind) 79,
80, 86–87, 88–89

dreams 20–22, 40; Scherner's
observations on 40; unconscious
wishes 21–22

Dresden Opera House, Germany
(Semper) 20

Educatorium (Koolhaas/OMA) 16,
93–95, 100–102, 103, 105, 106,
107; agencies of superego 102;
institutional spaces 93; open social-
mixer areas 93, 94; plan layout *94*;
regime rooms 102; social spaces 93

ego 47; differentiation 59; id and 57;
identifications 57, 59; phases of
development and 57; as selfhood 57;
see also superego

The Ego and the Id (Freud) 8, 57, 59,
61, 98

Eisenman, Peter 15; "House II" 68,
75–78

empathy 40; for closed-form
architectural objects 68, 72–78;
for critical simulation 81–90; for
formlessness 54–55, 62–67; for space
relationships 56; for spaces of social
encounter 16, 92, 95, 100–103;
theory 14, 41

erotic traits/types 98, 99

"The Essence of Architectural Creation"
(Schmarsow) 40

The Eyes of the Skin (Pallasmaa) 2

fantasy *see* phantasy

female patients and Freud 23

Fin-De-Siècle Vienna: Politics and Culture
(Schorske) 18, 34

"Findings, Ideas, Problems" (Freud) 4

The Flowers of Evil (Baudelaire) 26

Ford, Henry 22

Form Follows Libido (Lavin) 48

formless/formlessness 54–57; Moholy-Nagy's "space relationships" drawing 15, 54, *55*, 55–57, 63, 87; preferences and preoccupations with 64; Rebstockpark masterplan (Eisenman) 51, 54, 62–66; selfhood 63–64

free associations 72

free clinics 10

Freud: Charcot and 26–27; criticisms 22, 23; "Dora" case 23; early life 17; family circumstances 17; female patients 23; free clinics 10; introductory lectures 6; modern popular culture 1; social influence 22; spatialities of the psychical apparatus 57–58; system of thought 2, 17; writings 7, 23–24; *see also specific work*

Freud, Anna 6

Freud, Ernst 10

The Freud Reader (Gay) 7

frontal lobe 9

The Function of the Orgasm (Reich) 48

Gay, Peter 23

gender bias 23

generalized anxiety disorder 31

genital phase 16, 58, 92, 95–100; demands on the mind 96; repression in 95–96; search for obtainable objects 95; spaces of social encounter and 100–103; superego 59–60,

98, 99; threshold practices 96–97; transformations in 98; transition to adulthood 95; *see also* Educatorium (Koolhaas/OMA)

genital self-stimulation 83

Gestalt psychology 3

Giedion, Sigfried 15, 37, 38, 42–43

gift 69, 70; compliance and noncompliance behaviors 75; control of 15, 25, 68, 72–75; design composition as 74; self-promotional strategies to exhibit 74–75

Harlem Renaissance 35

Haussmann, Georges-Eugène 26, 27

Heidegger, Martin 2

helplessness 31–32

Herman, Judith 32

historical time periods 5–6

Holmes, Lucille 11

house(s): birth and 48; Neutra's design thinking 48–50

House II (Eisenman) 68, 75–78; criticality 77–78; diagrams 68, *69*, 76–77; as gift 75; repetition 77–78

hysteria 26–31; "Dora" case 23

id 98; ego 57; elementary instinctual demands 99; impulses of 57, 98; pleasure seeking impulses 57

ideational isolation 77

ideational representatives 76; *see also* decontamination

identity choice 1

impulses 58–59, 96–98; anal phase 68, 69, 71, 72; id 57, 98; phallic phase 82; projection 58; troubling 58
Inhibitions, Symptoms, and Anxiety (Freud) 97
interior space 41
The Interpretation of Dreams (Freud) 1, 18, 19, 20–22, 24, 40
"Introductory Lectures on Psychoanalysis" (Freud) 6
isolation strategies 71, 72
Italian Renaissance architecture 46

Kant, Immanuel 2
Klein, Melanie 45–46, 47, 70
Klimt, Gustav 21
Koolhaas, Rem 16, 51, 52, 53, 92, 93–94, 100, 101, 104, 105; on delirium of paranoia 50, 51; material culture of Manhattan 50

latency phase of psychical development 58
Lavin, Sylvia 48
Le Corbusier Oeuvre Complete (Boesiger) 74
libidinal traits/types 98, 99
The Life of the Dream (Scherner) 40
literal *vs.* phenomenal transparency 3–4
The Lives of the Most Excellent Painters, Sculptors, and Architects (Vasari) 85
Loos, Adolf 10

Mallgrave, Harry 9
manic position 45

marketing campaigns 1
Marx, Karl 22
masturbation *see* genital self-stimulation
memories 27–30; screen 14, 28–29, 30, 35, 36; traumatic 27–30
mental apparatus 57
Merleau-Ponty, Jacques 2
The Metropolis and Mental Life (Simmel) 20
modeling 46
modern architecture 19–20, 37, 52; self-promotional materials 74–75
Modern Architecture (Wagner) 19
modernity 22
Moholy-Nagy, László 15, 43–44, 51, 54–57, 63, 87
Moore House (Neutra) 48, 49

NAAB Conditions for Accreditation (2014) 32
narcissistic traits 1, 98–99
neurasthenia 26
neuroscience 8–9
neurosis 11, 20, 26, 30, 51–52, 62, 71; disorders representing 26; popular culture 26, 27; spatial 52; treatment 49
Neutra, Richard 10, 13, 48–50
"New Introductory Lectures" (Freud) 6
The New Vision (Moholy-Nagy) 43, 56
New York Athletic Club tower 50
NTR Headquarters (MVRDV) 102–103

objects 13; aesthetic identification with 40; empathy theorists 39; Freud's relationship with 17; identifications with 40, 99; phallic 83; *see also* aesthetic experience/intuition; phases of psychical development

obsessional trait/type 98, 99

obsessive and compulsive behaviors 71, 96

obsessive-compulsive disorders 72

oceanic feeling 14–15

oedipal complex/constraints 95–97

oedipal regime space 101

oedipal revolt 18

"On the Optical Sense of Form" (Vischer) 40

open form 4, 37, 42, 105,106; *see also* formless/formlessness

open-slab *vs.* regime room 100–103; *see also* Educatorium (Koolhaas/OMA)

oral phase of development 14–15, 58, 60–61; ego and 60, 61; mother's breast as object 60; self-image 60

Oxford English Dictionary 73–74

Pallasmaa, Juhani 2

Paris, France 26–27

Penguin Books 7

personal pronouns 1

phallic phantasy 87–90; concept 15–16; daydreaming and 84; genital self-stimulation 83; ideational contents 83; object of affection 83; reality *vs.* 83–84; selfhood and 81; unconscious

resistances to 84; "Vertical Horizon" (Libeskind) and 87–90; wish fulfillment 82, 83; *see also* "Vertical Horizon" (Libeskind)

phallic phase of development 15–16, 58, 81–84; genital self-stimulation 83; impulses of 82; parent as special object of affection 83; popular culture 83; selfhood and 81; wish fulfillment 82, 83

phallus 83

phantasy 45, 47, 70; as a psychoanalytic term 15–16, 82; spiteful 45; *see also* phallic phantasy

phantasy simulation 90

phases of psychical development 7–8, 58–60; anal phase 15, 58, 68–72; genital phase 16, 58, 92, 95–100; impulses 58–59, 96–98; latency 58; oral phase 14–15, 58, 60–61; phallic 15–16, 58, 81–84; sense of self in 96

phenomenal transparency 5; literal transparency *vs.* 3–4

phenomenologists 2–3

physical threats to selfhood 24

Plato 85

"Playtime" (film) 102

pleasure principle 98

political behavior 20

post-traumatic stress disorder 31, 33

principle of dressing 14, 39, 40

Principles of Art History (Wölfflin) 41, 42

Principles of Physiological Psychology (Wundt) 41

prohibitions and taboos 95; case of "Little Hans" 97; oedipal 97–98; phallic object 83; self-imposed and self-disciplinary 97

projection of impulses 58

Prolegomena to a Psychology of Architecture (Wölfflin) 37, 41

psyche: aesthetic preferences and 5; divisions 57; id 98; as internal structure/apparatus 13; outward projection 13

psychical apparatus, spatialities of 57–58

psychical development phases *see* phases of psychical development

psychical dispositions *see* dispositions

psychical ideas 57–58

psychoanalytic theory 6, 8–9

psychological threats to selfhood 24

"The Psychopathologies of Modern Space: Metropolitan Fear from Agoraphobia to Estrangement" (Vidler) 52

The Psychopathology of Everyday Life (Freud) 28, 30

psychotherapy clinic 10

The Quattro Cento (Stokes) 46–47

racial unconscious 35

racism 14; screen memories 35; unconscious memories 35

random thoughts 72

Rank, Otto 48, 49

reaction formations 71

reality *vs.* phallic phantasy 83–84

Rebstockpark masterplan (Eisenman) 51, 54; blurred zones 54, 62–66, *63, 65*; freestanding slab 62; slab-forms 62, 66; solids and voids 62, 66; temporal modulations 66; 3-dimensional matrix design 51, 65–66, *66*

The Redesign of Studio Culture 32

regime room *vs.* open slab 100–103; *see also* Educatorium (Koolhaas/OMA)

Reich, Wilhelm 10, 48

Remembering, Repeating, and Working Through (Freud) 29–30

Renaissance 46, 86

reparation 45–46, 47

repetition 71, 77–78; unconscious wishes 78

repression 61–62, 70, 95–96; concept 61; ego identification 61; ideational chains of association 61–62

"Repression" (Freud) 61

The Republic (Plato) 85

Ringstrasse, Vienna 18, 19

Rourke House (Neutra) 48

Rowe, Colin 3–4, 37

rule-based composition 72–75

Salpêtrière building, Paris 26–27

Schmarsow, August 40–41, 43–44

Schopenhauer, Arthur 42, 43–44

Schorske, C. 18, 19, 20–21, 34

science and psychoanalysis 23

screen memories 14, 28–29, 30, 35, 36

self-centered tendencies 1

self-determination 2

selfhood 1–2, 21; early-modern interest in 18; emancipatory promises 23–24; formless-form of 63–64; psychical 22–24; thick *vs.* thin view 6; threats to 24, 33

self-promotional strategies of architects 74–75

Semper, Gottfried 14, 20, 37, 38–39, 41, 53, 92; principle of dressing 14, 39, 40; *Style in the Technical and Tectonic Arts* 38–39

sensory organs 21

sexual experience 21

sexuality in arts 18

sexual preference 1

shell shock 24, 30–31

Simmel, George 20

simulation 79–90; overview 15–16, 79; phallic role 81; "Vertical Horizon" (Libeskind) 16, 79–81, 85–91; virtual space 79; wishful ideas 84–85

Sitte, Camillo 19, 20, 26, 37, 38, 94

Slutzky, Robert 3–4, 37

social distancing 105–106

social media 1, 106–107

space creation 40–41, 87

space relationship, Moholy-Nagy's drawing of 15, 44, 54, *55*, 55–57, 63, 87

spaces of social encounter 92–103; Educatorium 16, 93–95, *94*, 100–103; freedom and constraint 16, 93–95, 100–103; open slab *vs.* regime room 100–103; overview 16

spatialities of psychical apparatus 57–58

The Standard Edition of the Complete Psychological Works of Sigmund Freud (Stratchey and Freud) 6–7

Stokes, Adrian 44–47

Stones of Rimini (Stokes) 44–45, 46

students, studio culture and 24–25, 33–34

Studies on Hysteria (Freud and Breuer) 25–26, 27, 30

studio culture 24–25, 33–34

Style in the Technical and Tectonic Arts (Semper) 38–39

subjectivity, early-modern interest in 18

subtractive composition 74

superego 59–60, 102; genital phase 59, 98, 99; as locus of reaction formations 59; thought and avoidance behaviors 60

symbolic communication 39

Tati, Jacques 102

technology 19, 94

temptations 72

Thom, Rene 66

Three Essays on the Theory of Sexuality (Freud) 8, 21, 58, 68, 82, 95, 96, 104

threshold practices 71–72, 96–97; isolation strategies 71; repetition strategies 71

"The Transformation of Instinct…" (Freud) 61

trauma 24–35; affirmation 32, 35; anxiety and 33; awareness about 24; birth 48, 49; concept 24;

cultural contexts 35; disconnection 32–33; generalized anxiety disorder 31; inability to avoid threat and helplessness 31–32; shell shock 24, 30–31; understanding 24–25

Trauma and Recovery (Herman) 32

"The Uncanny" (Freud) 52

unconscious 8–9, 37, 51; collective 35; racial 35; *see also* aesthetic experience/intuition

"The Unconscious" (Freud) 61

unconscious memories *see* screen memories

unconscious motivations 5

unconscious wishes 12; affirmation of 12; dreams 21–22; obsessive and compulsive behaviors 96; repetition 78

urban space 52

US National Architecture Accreditation Board (NAAB) 25

US Veteran's Administration 31

Vasari, Giorgio 85

"Vertical Horizon" (Libeskind) 16, 79–81, 85–91; architectonic elements 89; architectural affection 79; architecture *vs.* not-architecture beliefs 86–87; drawings 79, *80*, 86–87, 88–89; as ideational representative of unconscious phallic

impulses 85–86, 87; orthographic conventions 79, 89; oxymoronic drawing 88; as a phallic object 89; phallic phantasy and 87–90; phantasy simulation 90; style conventions 85; as taboo 85–86

Vesely, Dalibor 85

Vidler, Anthony 52

Vienna 9, 17–22, 26; architectural preferences 19–20; free clinics 10; psychoanalysis 13–14; reactionary politics 21; Ringstrasse 18, 19; zeitgeist 93, 94

Vietnam War 31

Villa VPRO (MVRDV) 102–103

Vischer, Robert 14, 40

visual experience of building facades 3

Wagner, Otto 19, 20, 37, 38, 94

Warped Space (Vidler) 52

Wölfflin, Heinrich 37, 38, 39, 41–43, 52, 73

The World as Will and Representation (Schopenhauer) 42

Wright, Richard 14, 35

Wundt, Wilhelm 41, 42

WWI 25, 30, 31

WWII 31, 32

Zaretsky, Eli 23–24, 35

zeitgeist 93, 94